D1169950

WHAT the

BEST

CEOs

KNOW

7 Exceptional Leaders and
Their Lessons for Transforming
any Business

JEFFREY A. KRAMES

McGraw-Hill

New York   St. Louis   San Francisco   Washington, D.C.   Auckland
Bogotá   Caracas   Lisbon   London   Madrid   Mexico City
Milan   Montreal   New Delhi   San Juan   Singapore
Sydney   Tokyo   Toronto

567890 DOC/DOC 0987   (PBK)
34567890 DOC/DOC 09876543 (HC)

ISBN 0-07-146252-X (PBK)
ISBN 0-07-138240-2 (HC)

First McGraw-Hill paperback edition published in 2005.

McGraw-Hill books are available at special quantity discounts to use as premiums and sales promotions, or for use in corporate training programs. For more information, please write to the Director of Special Sales, Professional Publishing, McGraw-Hill, Two Penn Plaza, New York, NY 10121-2298. Or contact your local bookstore.

Permission to use quoted material is as follows:

Chapter 5: From *Only the Paranoid Survive* by Andrew S. Grove, copyright © 1996 by Andrew S. Grove. Used by permission of Doubleday, a division of Random House, Inc., and HarperCollins Publishers Ltd.

Chapter 7: From *NUTS! Southwest Airlines' Crazy Recipe for Business and Personal Success* by Kevin and Jackie Freiberg. www.SDCGInc.com.

Chapter 8: From *Sam Walton: Made in America* by Sam Walton, copyright © 1992 by the Estate of Samuel Moore Walton. Used by permission of Doubleday, a division of Random House, Inc.

To my parents, who turned a small apartment in the Bronx into a learning organization of their own

And to my incredible wife, for her unending patience and encouragement. An author, and husband, has never had a better partner.

CONTENTS

v

The Era of the CEO?

The late 1990s and early 2000s brought seismic changes to corporate America and U.S. financial markets—changes that shook our collective confidence in several of our most important institutions.

Since much of the work that went into this book took place in that tumultuous period, the events that played out during those years (roughly 1998 through mid-2002) had a substantial impact on the shape and content of the book. What started out as a straightforward task of chronicling the business tactics and methods of a small group of successful CEOs became a far more complex challenge.

When I began writing this book, the business environment could not have looked much better. In the late 1990s, the U.S. stock markets were riding high, having enjoyed almost two decades of unprecedented and nearly uninterrupted growth. The Dow Jones Industrial Average, which at the start of the bull market in 1982 had hovered at around 800, had broken through both the 10,000- and 11,000-point psychological barriers. (Pundits were then prognosticating about the Dow soaring to *30,000* in the not-too-distant future!) The tech-heavy NASDAQ Index, meanwhile, was on an even more breathtaking ride up to the 5000-point level. In a display of hubris that seems quaint in retrospect, the NASDAQ had begun calling itself the stock exchange of the next century.

This upsurge in market valuations had profound effects on the investing public—the base of which had also grown enormously as defined-contribution retirement plans replaced defined-benefit plans. (Several decades ago, only a small percentage of Americans owned individual stocks or shares in mutual funds. Today, approximately 60 percent of U.S. households do.) Simply put, a lot more of us had a lot more of our assets in the markets, and we were doing well. In the words of Fed Chairman Alan Greenspan, a "wealth effect" took hold: We felt richer, so we spent more, and the economy climbed to new heights. The so-called new economy promised even more riches in the years ahead.

Popular historian Frederick Lewis Allen once referred to the 1920s as an "entrepreneurial riot." The same could be said about the later 1980s and the 1990s. Business was king, and business leaders such as Microsoft's Bill Gates and GE's Jack Welch were idealized, and even idolized. In the summer of 2000, a publisher paid more than $7 million for the right to publish Jack Welch's memoirs. This was a record advance for a business book and a near-record advance for a nonfiction book (only the pope had had a richer payday, until both Clintons eclipsed that level later).

It was a heady time for corporate America, and just about everyone caught a touch of the fever. New business and finance magazines hit the stands, and we snapped them up. Cable financial news programs—even whole networks— came into being, and we gave them good ratings. Successful mutual fund managers, who in earlier years would have labored in near-total anonymity, became the financial equivalent of pop stars. (Who was as well known as Peter Lynch before Peter Lynch?) But the brightest stars in the business firmament were those top-tier CEOs. Their pictures were emblazoned on the covers of books and magazines, and they weighed in on the important issues of the day.

I must confess that despite my role as a skeptical observer in a cutthroat industry (publishing), I was not immune to the euphoria, or even above a little hero worship.

When the financial newspaper *Barron's* asked me to write a piece on Jack Welch, the piece was entitled "The Price of Heroes," and it included the phrase "American icon" in the subtitle. When *Newsweek* asked me for a comment on Welch's book deal (which was not concluded by my own company, I should add), I observed that advances in excess of $5 million "used to be reserved for the Oval Office, now they are going to the corner office."

In 1997 and again in 1999, *Time* chose a CEO as its Person of the Year (Andy Grove of Intel and Jeff Bezos of Amazon, respectively). This distinction was normally the turf of potentates and ultra-celebrities; now it was being given to entrepreneurs and chief executives.

But inevitably, the party ended. Some of the people we had been celebrating—Andy Grove among them—turned out to have been just as visionary and influential as we had made them out to be. Others did not. Some of those hot companies—certainly Microsoft, and probably Amazon—turned out to have staying power and the ability to create value over the long run. But most did not. By the end of 2001, the vast majority of the high-flying dot-com companies had crashed and burned, sparking the greatest swoon of any financial market in history. The NASDAQ, which had enjoyed 3 years of record growth, fell from a high of more than 5000 in March of 2000 to under 1200 by the fall of 2002.

Almost everything is obvious in retrospect. From the vantage point of early 2003, it's easy to see the lessons of this strange period in American business history. Very few of those lessons are new, or even that surprising. For example, *"A soaring stock price alone does not a business make."* A viable business requires a viable business model that is capable of producing a respectable revenue stream. This was true in the days of Carnegie and Morgan, and it remains true to this day.

When the new-economy house of cards came tumbling down, the reverberations were profound and far-reaching. The precipitous drop of the NASDAQ, for example, helped push thousands of businesses under water. It also wiped out *trillions of dollars* of shareholder value, destroying the nest eggs of many millions of individual investors. (The phenomenon was not restricted to the United States; Europe and Asia were hit even harder.) And this was only the first of many heavy shoes that were dropping on an already stunned investing public.

CEOS IN THE CROSSHAIRS

There is much talk today that the organization is the enemy of the individual, and that while all organizations are enemies of sorts, the archenemy is undoubtedly the business organization.

This quote sounds like it was written yesterday. In fact, it appeared in the pages of *Fortune* more than four decades ago. I include it here to underscore the fact that we have often regarded corporations and their leaders with a certain amount of suspicion.

At the time of this writing, several scandals are continuing to unfold across corporate America, torching the image of both corporations and the individuals who lead them. Companies like Enron, Global Crossing, Tyco, Adelphia, and WorldCom have become evil icons, and their fall from grace has inevitably cast a pall over the reputation of the once-heralded chief executive. In June 2002, the *New York*

Times made it official, declaring on its front page that "The Imperial Chief Executive Is Suddenly in the Cross Hairs." In December 2002, *U.S. News & World Report* named former Tyco CEO Dennis Kozlowski its "Rogue of the Year" for typifying corporate "sleaze." Kozlowski, purchaser of the infamous $6000 shower curtain, allegedly misappropriated $600 million from Tyco's coffers. Even the queen of good living, Martha Stewart, found herself at the center of an alleged insider trading scandal.

Politicians responded to the scandals with a predictable array of public postures, ranging from outrage to befuddlement. President Bush vowed to "hold people accountable," but members of his own administration (including himself) were not all that far removed from the kinds of shenanigans that were showing up on the front pages. As for the business world, it was Andy Grove who best summed up the feelings of many: "I've been in business for 40 years," he commented, "[but lately] I find myself feeling embarrassed and ashamed" to be a businessman.

Of course, the vast majority of CEOs were—and are—law-abiding citizens who work hard to achieve their organizational objectives, which almost always include making an honest living. And few newspapers print stories about CEOs doing the right things. For example, in the wake of September 11, Dell Computer held many town meetings with its employees, contributed hundreds of computers to the New York City mayor's office and the recovery site, and donated millions of dollars to the Red Cross (from places as far away as Dell Germany). Dell also did some important work for the Pentagon, and for that act was given a special recognition award by a U.S. Army general in Austin. Michael Dell spoke of how performing these acts was "extremely powerful for people in terms of feeling like they actually could do something that was meaningful."

But these sorts of deeds were of little comfort to those Americans who were seeing their 401(k) plans and stock portfolios shrink dramatically. The numbers were truly staggering. More than *one million* Americans who had already retired, or who had planned to do so imminently, were forced to go back into (or remain in) the workforce in 2001 and 2002, after their retirement nest eggs went up in smoke.

It's no surprise, then, that the Age of the Celebrity CEO ended abruptly. We love our heroes, but we also love it when they reveal their feet of clay. The demise of the celebrity CEO was accelerated, and sealed, by the first images of executives being taken off in handcuffs—pictures that appeared in virtually every newspaper in the country. Those first arrests (and the subsequent efforts at punishment and restitution) were cheered by Main Street and more or less tolerated by Wall Street. The public demanded that someone be held accountable, and someone certainly would be.

No CEO was above the wave of outrage that was then cresting—not even the man named by *Fortune* as Manager of the Century. In late September of 2002, Jack Welch found himself at the center of a number of controversies that threatened to tarnish his image permanently. Months earlier, the *Wall Street Journal* had broken the story of Welch's extramarital affair, and the revelation precipitated a bitter divorce case.

When the proceedings of that case were made public, it was revealed that Welch's retirement package from GE included a $15 million apartment, laundry service, first-class tickets to sporting events, use of the company jet, and endless other perks. In a column in the *Wall Street Journal*, Welch lamented that the court filing "grossly misrepresented" many aspects of his employment contract. In the same column, Welch announced that he would reimburse the company for the perks he had received since his retirement, and would pay for them in the future. (Soon after, the Securities and Exchange Commission revealed that it was conducting an informal investigation into Welch's pay package.)

The story lingered, nevertheless, because the hero's warts were on full display. Welch's business strategies—and the quality of GE's earnings—were called into question for the first time in years. GE's stock price fell faster than the stock market as a whole in the year following Welch's departure. Newspapers and magazines ran several prominent stories about how the mighty had fallen, and described Welch's fading legacy.

From his public utterances, it's clear that Welch understood that just as he had been a beneficiary of the great bull market, he was now the victim of a new, "post-Enron" corporate fallout. The rules had changed. In a soaring stock market, the press (and investors) took little notice of a multimillion-dollar postretirement pay package. But now, deals cut in the quiet of the boardroom could lead to raucous public controversy, and even the most successful leaders could expect scrutiny.

Executive compensation packages in particular emerged as a natural target, given the fact that the pay levels of large-company chief executives had soared to astronomical levels, contributing to the growing disparity between the corner office and the corner cubicle. According to *Fortune*, between 1970 and 1999, the average real compensation of the top 100 CEOs leaped from 39 times that of the average employee to more than 1000 times that of the average worker! And although it's far too early to write the final assessment of Jack Welch and his ilk, it seems clear that their reputations are now at risk of being consumed by the same "celebrity machine" that helped to create them.

That would be too bad. You can make a strong case that Welch's compensation was excessive, and that there is a considerable gap between his professional prescriptions and his personal behavior. But his record as a business leader is indisputable. Under his direction, GE was transformed from an out-of-touch, $25 billion industrial manufacturer into an agile, $130 billion service juggernaut. Recognizing the limits of the command-and-control hierarchies that ruled the day, Welch remade one of the world's largest bureaucracies into an organization that had learning and ideas at its heart.

And Welch is not alone. I would argue that when we begin to dismiss all CEOs and business leaders as dishonest or greedy, we are being self-indulgent. We put ourselves at risk of throwing out the baby with the bathwater. There *are* important lessons still to be learned from certain business leaders, even in an era when business is in disrepute.

The seven leaders profiled in this book are indisputably in that category. No, they are not flawless. They all made mistakes, and most of them came under fire at one time or another for everything from strategic missteps to monopolistic business tactics and, yes, excessive pay packages.

But missteps aside, these people were *builders*. They created legacies that include some of the most innovative business ideas and concepts of the last decades of the twentieth century. To ignore their accomplishments and overlook the business lessons inherent in those accomplishments would be a serious mistake.

Who are they? Here's the final list:

- Michael Dell (founder and CEO, Dell Computer)

- Jack Welch (former CEO, GE)

- Lou Gerstner (former CEO, IBM)

- Andy Grove (cofounder and former CEO, Intel)

- Bill Gates (cofounder and former CEO, Microsoft)

- Herb Kelleher (founder and former CEO, Southwest Airlines)

- Sam Walton (founder and former CEO, Wal-Mart)

This book is by no means a tribute to the individuals profiled, any one of whom may yet turn out to have feet of clay. (This tends to happen a lot when the rules of the game change.) Instead, it is intended to spotlight their insights, ideas, and innovations, and to show how these can be applied in almost any organization.

At the time of this writing, only one of my seven subject CEOs (Michael Dell) still holds that title. Five others have either retired or taken on a different title, and one (Sam Walton) has died. But I believe that their ideas are as relevant today as they were when they were pioneered years ago. Their companies endure; more important, the *concepts* behind those companies will be studied and emulated by managers for decades to come.

A READER'S GUIDE TO
WHAT THE BEST CEOs KNOW

While this book will provide some historical context for each of the companies and CEOs discussed within it, I haven't tried to write a business history, or even a sustained narrative. Instead, I've tried to create an easy-to-follow road map that will not only help managers and aspiring managers understand the traits and strategies of these successful leaders, but also show them how to apply these traits and strategies to their own organizations.

The first part of the book, "What Made Them Great," consists of a single chapter that is intended to accomplish two goals: (1) to explain the criteria that I used to choose the CEOs for inclusion in this book, and (2) to identify and discuss the defining traits and/or accomplishments that these leaders had in common. While not every CEO excelled in every one of the areas identified, each of the traits identified in this chapter can be found in the majority of the seven CEOs.

For example, one of the hallmarks of exceptional CEOs is their willingness to implement within their own organizations the *very best ideas out there*, regardless of where those ideas originated. The late Sam Walton, for example, created Wal-Mart by studying competitors and doing what they did—only *better*. Later, that behavior would be the key to developing a learning culture. In the 1990s, Jack Welch took the concept of a learning culture to a new and previously unexplored level by creating one of the world's largest learning organizations, involving a myriad of diverse global businesses.

Part 2 of the book, "Defining Strategies of Exceptional Leaders," includes seven chapters devoted to the CEOs and their signature strategies. The focus of each of these chapters is on introducing the leader's key strategy, explaining it and its origin in depth, and showing how it can be applied in other organizations or situations. To achieve this, and also to help the reader "think like a leader," each chapter includes the following:

- **WHAT WOULD [THE CEO] DO?** Each chapter begins with a brief scenario that puts the reader in the seat of the CEO. A business situation set within a particular industry is briefly described, usually in two pages. In these cases, the readers get the chance to test their business acumen against that of each of the seven subject CEOs.

  At the conclusion of the case, the reader is encouraged to decide on a particular course of action. The case ends with the question "What would Michael Dell do?" (or Jack Welch, Herb Kelleher, and so on). The business scenario is placed at the beginning of the chapter to challenge readers, stimulate their thinking, and put them in the proper mind-set. Each is in a sense a quiz, but not a disqualifying quiz. Since the clues to "passing" each quiz are included in each chapter, I hope that they will be intriguing and even entertaining. And I hope that by the end of each chapter, the appropriate course of action—or at least *an* appropriate course of action—will be more apparent.

One disclaimer: To make a point, I may describe a situation that stretches the limits of business reality (although only by a little bit, in most cases). So please suspend disbelief and grant me some poetic license. My goal is not to immerse you in the dynamics of seven industries or businesses with 100 percent accuracy. Instead, I want to paint a business situation in broad brushstrokes in order to stimulate your thoughts and responses.

Furthermore, while no one (probably even including the leaders themselves) knows exactly how these leaders would respond to the particular hypothetical challenge presented to them, I suggest one solution at the end of each chapter. These proposed solutions are possible and plausible, in my opinion, and reflect my understanding of how each of the subject CEOs has tackled similar problems in the past. You are entirely free to come up with better answers.

- **EVERY CHAPTER HAS LESSONS THROUGHOUT.** In addition to the lessons inherent in these cases and their solutions, each chapter also includes other kinds of lessons at regular intervals. These are usually placed at the end of a section to emphasize a particular insight or leadership action. The point of these editorial asides, as you might expect, is to help translate ideas from a specific industry context to a larger context and to suggest how the knowledge presented in that section can be applied by managers in other organizations.

- EACH CHAPTER HAS "ASSESS YOUR CEO QUOTIENT" QUES-
  TIONS. The "solution" to the case or scenario ("What
  Would Michael Dell Do") at the end of the chapter is
  followed by a brief (and unscientific) assessment exercise. It is intended not only to help readers gauge their
  own leadership abilities vis-à-vis each of the business
  leaders profiled, but also to put the reader's *organization* to the test—to ascertain whether or not the organization employs the practices of each of the CEOs.

- MORE LESSONS FOLLOW THE ASSESSMENT. The chapter
  concludes with several additional ideas for implementing the strategies discussed in the chapter.

- SELECTED CHAPTERS INCLUDE THOUGHTS FROM BUSI-
  NESS THEORISTS such as Peter Drucker and Philip
  Kotler. The point of this is to study the CEOs' strategies or tactics from another viewpoint, and to add insight into a particular strategy or concept.

PART 1

What Made Them Great

CHAPTER 1

The Exceptional Seven and the Traits That Defined Them

The seven CEOs featured in this book were selected on the basis of research that I conducted over a 4-year period. This research—which added up to several hundred hours of study and analysis, all told—included interviews with CEOs, interviews with experts such as Northwestern's marketing guru Philip Kotler (who provided enlightening insights on my material), and a careful review of literally hundreds of books, articles, speeches, annual reports, web sites, stock charts, and so on.

While very specific criteria were employed to narrow down the list to the final seven, there was a subjective element to the selection process as well. As the editor and publisher of more than 250 business books, I have edited works that documented the lives and insights of such business leaders as William Paley (founder of CBS), Michael Eisner (Disney), Michael Ovitz (founder of Creative Artists and later president of Disney), Jack Welch (GE), about whom I also wrote a book, Ross Perot (founder of EDS), and Lou Gerstner (IBM), among others. It was, of course, impossible not to form opinions of these individuals as I studied them and learned about their accomplishments. This was good background, but it was also a potential source of bias. I attempted to counteract any such bias by studying other business leaders about whose careers I had no special knowledge.

When this project began, the list of possible CEOs numbered more than three dozen. The final list was determined fairly late in the process—in the spring of 2002, when the initial research phase of the book was complete. Without naming names, I will confess that I wrote partial (and sometimes complete) chapters about other individuals who, for one reason or another, failed to make the final cut. In some cases, these also-rans fell victim to the hard times that followed the turn of the century. (They didn't survive professionally, or their organizations were acquired or merged.) But more often, they fell off the list because I learned that, strong reputations notwithstanding, they did not meet the criteria for inclusion. Yes, they were accomplished in their own way, but their accomplishments did not seem to speak as loudly as their reputations, or did not promise to apply across a broad spectrum of business situations.

HOW THE CEOs WERE SELECTED

The seven CEOs depicted in this book represent the best of a breed of managers who were shaped, in part, by the conditions and challenges that characterized the post-1980 business environment. Several factors changed the rules of the game in the 1980s: intense foreign competition (from Europe and Japan, most notably) and a technological environment that continuously shifted the landscape, demanding that managers and corporations adapt to the new lightning-paced arena. These sweeping changes required a new type of business leader, one who would *embrace* change, rather than deny or resist it.

These leaders understood the necessity of creating enterprises that were strong enough and resilient enough to weather storms and/or downturns. For example, as the CEO of one of the lowest-priced airlines in the industry, Herb Kelleher built a company that he knew would perform well in good times and bad. Jack Welch formulated his "number one, number two" strategy, which called for all GE businesses to be either number one or number two in their respective markets. This was one of the strategies that defined the GE chairman's approach: He believed strongly that any business that was not one of the top two in its industry would fare poorly during market setbacks.

The leaders in this book knew that "business as usual" was most likely a prescription for failure. For example, Sam Walton founded Wal-Mart in 1962 because he recognized the need to compete with a new type of retailer or risk being rendered irrelevant. He saw no reason why people who lived in small towns could not get the same low prices as people who lived in much larger cities. He was not the first discounter, of course, but the story of how he built the company from a small, 16,000-square-foot store in Rogers, Arkansas (with no fixtures, only tables!), into the world's largest company provides important lessons for other managers and organizations.[1]

Andy Grove's bold move in 1985 is another case of a CEO striking out in a new direction as a result of a quickly shifting competitive marketplace. His decision to get out of the memory chip business—the business upon which the company was founded—shocked even Intel insiders. But Grove had come to the conclusion that he and his colleagues had no choice. And contained in that single painful decision were the seeds of the company's future success, as the company went on to become the world's preeminent producer of microprocessors.

---

[1] In 2002, Wal-Mart became the largest company in the world in terms of sales volume, at $218 billion.

Like Grove, most of the leaders featured in this book recognized the massive changes that were reshaping their industries and affecting their companies' future. Having developed this clear-eyed vision, they then devised strategies and tactics that would help their corporations not only weather the storm, but also emerge as industry leaders. These are the leaders whose ideas and actions fill the pages of this book.

The criteria for final inclusion in the book consisted of three deciding factors:

1. EACH CEO LED A COMPANY THAT WAS A MARKET LEADER AND/OR THAT OUTPERFORMED ITS PEERS. Several metrics were used to select the initial list of CEOs, including the revenues, stock market performance, and growth rate of the companies they led. I sought to identify companies and CEOs that were market leaders in a number of different industries or industry niches. Generating an initial list was relatively simple; paring it down, as noted, was more difficult. In some cases, closer scrutiny helped; in others, the passage of time was even more helpful. Some leaders on the initial list stumbled badly and proved unable to recover. This leads to my next criterion.

2. EACH OF THE CEOs' LEADERSHIP STRATEGIES STOOD THE TEST OF TIME. As mentioned previously, many CEOs were removed from the list when their companies faded. *Why* a company stumbled mattered a great deal. For example, if a company's market capitalization declined, but that decline correlated with a re-

cession or a sagging stock market, my potential subject was not automatically dropped from the list (although, as will be demonstrated shortly, the majority of the companies on the final list fared better than their peers during market downturns). In addition, most of the companies headed or founded by the seven CEOs performed well *even after the CEO stepped down*. Sam Walton died in 1992, but the success of Wal-Mart in the decade following his death is testament to the enduring quality of his vision.

3. **EACH OF THE CEOS CONTRIBUTED TO THE BODY OF MANAGEMENT KNOWLEDGE.** The truly exceptional CEOs—the ones who make it into the management textbooks—most often have pioneered an idea or technique that others could learn from. To put it conversely, unless a CEO came up with a construct that other managers and CEOs could apply, he wasn't included in this book, which, as stated earlier, is intended to provide a blueprint for other managers to learn from and use.

One final note on the selection of CEOs: In March 2002, *Fortune* issued its annual list of "America's Most Admired Companies." This is an interesting and meaningful survey, in my estimation, because it draws upon the opinions of 10,000 executives, directors, and security analysts, who are asked to select the 10 companies they admire the most.

In 2002, five of the companies once headed by CEOs profiled in this book were among the top 10 on this list. Heading the list was GE, followed by Southwest, Wal-

Mart, and Microsoft. Coming in at number 10 was Intel. (The previous year's survey had included these five plus Dell Computer at number 10. The only company represented in this book that did not make the *Fortune* list in either 2001 or 2002 was IBM; one would have to go back to 1987 to find IBM in the top 10.) *Fortune*'s list of "Global Most Admired Companies" included GE, Wal-Mart, and Microsoft in the top three positions, and Intel at number 7.

As noted earlier, most of the leaders included in this book no longer held the title of CEO by the year 2002. But the fact that five of the seven companies once headed by these executives appeared on these lists in 2001 and 2002 demonstrates the durability of these leaders' vision and/or strategies, as judged by their peers. My selection process was entirely independent of this survey (or any other). Nevertheless, I take the substantial overlap between my list and *Fortune*'s to be a form of independent validation. I reached my conclusions by one path, and *Fortune* reached its conclusions by another, but we got to more or less the same place.

GREAT COMPANIES, GREAT INVESTMENTS?

Shareholder returns are one of the most important metrics used to evaluate the performance of a publicly traded company—and, by extension, the CEO who heads it—over the long run. In their respective heydays, all of the companies run by the CEOs profiled in this book have enriched their shareholders over the long term (as indicated by the following charts, which show the stock market performance of these seven companies).

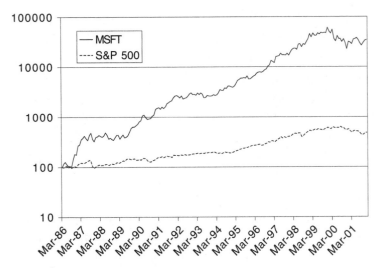

Microsoft

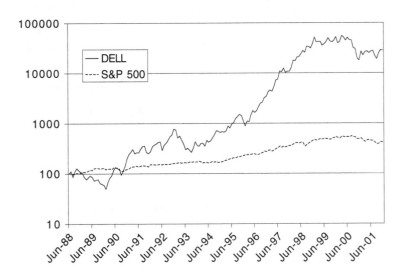

Dell

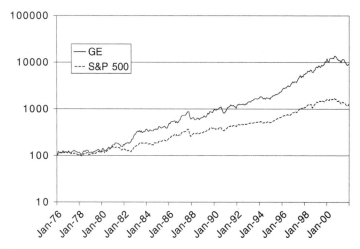

GE

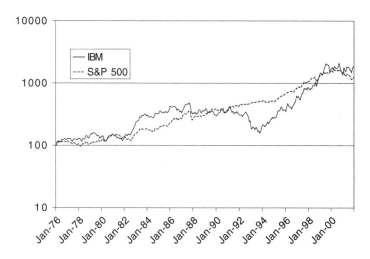

IBM

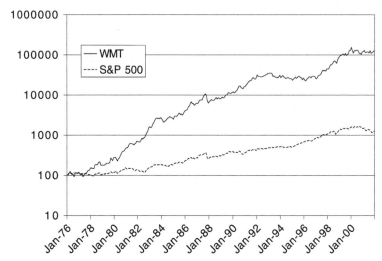

Wal–Mart

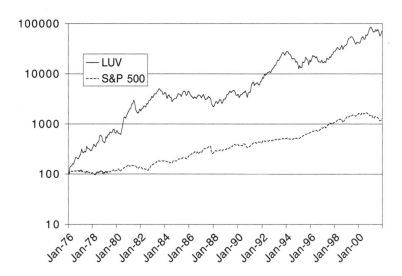

Southwest Airlines

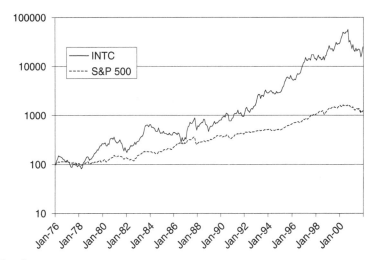

Intel

(Charts courtesy of Jeremy J. Siegel.)

For example, Bill Gates cofounded a company that for several brief periods, including late 2002, was the most valuable company in the world, beating out Jack Welch's GE. This is all the more remarkable given that Microsoft was one of the last of the seven companies to be founded (in 1976). The success of the company's stock made the moniker "Microsoft Millionaire" part of the business vernacular, particularly in the better neighborhoods around Seattle.

Michael Dell, of course, was responsible for *the* stock of the 1990s. During this decade, Dell's stock price soared an astronomical *89,000 percent*. During the great NASDAQ meltdown in the early 2000s, Dell held up better than most, and, as we will see, the company *increased its market share* during this difficult period.

Dell was exceptional, but he wasn't a complete anomaly. All but one of the CEOs in this book headed companies that outperformed their peers and the S&P 500 for long stretches of time in the 1980s and 1990s. Intel, Microsoft, and Wal-Mart, for example, trounced the S&P almost from the very beginning.

GE was also a star performer under Welch. When he became CEO, GE's annual revenues were about $25 billion. When he stepped down in 2001, they were about $130 billion. GE has grown at a rate of between 10 and 17 percent through all economic cycles since 1979. At the company's zenith, GE was worth some $596 billion, and its stock sold at a price-to-earnings multiple of 48, far outpacing the typical multiple for a blue-chip stock. On average, the GE's returns under Welch were *double* the average for the S&P.

The only company that had difficulty beating the S&P during the 1980s and 1990s was IBM. By the time Gerstner arrived at IBM in 1993, "Big Blue" was so deeply in the red that it took 5 years before IBM's returns outperformed the S&P 500, and then only by a slim margin. However, the turnaround was no small feat considering how deep a hole the company had dug for itself: In 1993, IBM had recorded an $8 billion loss, eclipsing the prior year's loss of $5 billion.

I think it important to inject a note of caution at this point. While market capitalization is a useful metric for evaluating the performance of a major corporation and its leaders, there is considerable risk in getting too wrapped up in financial measures. First, as we've seen all too frequently in recent months, these measures can be manipulated. Second, these measures are a sort of report card, a judgment on how well the organization and its leaders have played the game, but they are *not* the game itself.

John Bogle, one of the titans of the investing world, put it another way. Cautioning of the "perils of numeracy," he decreed "that today, in our society, in economics, and in finance, we place too much trust in numbers. Numbers are not reality. At best, they're a pale reflection of reality. At worst, they're a gross distortion of the truths we seek to measure." In light of those sagacious words, in this book, I want to focus on the strategies and tactics that lie behind, and contribute to, financial success.

For example, although Southwest Airlines became the leading discount airline in the United States, it has never been the largest. However, Herb Kelleher takes great pride in the fact that in the three-plus decades of its existence, Southwest has been the only airline never to have a losing year (including the year following September 11, 2001). But what he is probably *most* proud of is that Southwest has won the airline industry's coveted "Triple Crown"—best monthly on-time record, best baggage handling, and fewest customer complaints—*32 times*. If you're a frequent flyer, you know that this is an astounding record.

What was going on here? Kelleher told his people not to worry about profits. Instead, he said incessantly, *worry about service*, and everything else will fall into place. The marketplace proved him right, and rewarded his airline. In the fall of 2002, a year after the tragic terrorist attacks on the World Trade Center—which, among other outcomes, shook the airline industry to its core—the market capitalization of Southwest was eight times that of AMR, the parent company of American Airlines.

IN SEARCH OF THE LEADERSHIP THREADS

After finalizing my list, I subjected each of the leaders and the company he led to another kind of analysis. The goal of this exercise was different from that of the work that finalized the list of seven. The sole aim of this research was to identify the leadership threads that tied these CEOs together. In other words, what did these seven extraordinary leaders have in common? While there is some overlap between these criteria and the traits that narrowed the list, in this phase I subjected the seven identified leaders to even more scrutiny, and ultimately identified what I consider to be the keys to exceptional leadership.

Six characteristics and/or traits describe and connect the seven CEOs in this book:

1. THE BEST CEOS START WITH A VIEW OF THE MARKET- PLACE AND INSTILL AN "OUTSIDE-IN" PERSPECTIVE INTO THE COMPANY. In other words, the most effective CEOs start with a view of the market, then work back to create an organization focused on satisfying customer needs. The best example of this is Dell Computer, a company that puts the customer at the center of virtually everything it does.

   Michael Dell said that he did not create what became known as the direct model out of any great vision. That model, though, is what makes the company unique and has helped it expand into a $30 billion- plus organization. "The direct model has a number of attributes," Michael Dell stated. "Of course, being in touch with customer needs is one of its most fundamental." It is difficult to imagine a more customer-centric organization than Dell's, since each product is custom-ordered, and the company is structured around customers or customer groups.

One person who might disagree with that last sentence is David Glass, the man who worked with Sam Walton for decades and later succeeded him as chairman of Wal-Mart. Glass felt that one of the reasons Wal-Mart succeeded against long odds was Walton's fierce commitment to offering his customers the lowest prices, regardless of where they lived.

Sam Walton once said, "Every time Wal-Mart spends one dollar foolishly, it comes out of our customers' pockets." That sentiment is still deeply embedded in the psyche of the company, more than a decade after the founder's death. Glass, who led the company to even greater heights after Walton stepped down, said that he couldn't be Sam Walton. His task, he said, was to "build on his legacy and build on his philosophies and use all of those as strengths." Clearly, he succeeded in that task.

Lou Gerstner inherited a company that was anything but customer-centric. Gerstner said that the company "had lost touch with the marketplace and its customers." That explains why the company was losing so much money (and goes some distance toward explaining why at that time almost no self-respecting manager was willing to take the CEO job at IBM). When the company failed to grasp the personal computer revolution and other important changes within its industry, the stock fell below $15 for the first time since the early 1980s (when adjusted for subsequent stock splits). IBM badly needed someone who could put a customer mindset back into the company.

Here's how Gerstner viewed IBM when he looked back on the company in 2002:

> *In the spring of 1993, a big part of what I had to do was get the company refocused on the marketplace as the only valid measure of success. I started by telling virtually every audience I spoke to in the first couple of months that there was a customer running IBM, and that we were going to rebuild the company from the customer back. Those are pretty simple statements, but hugely important in reshaping the mindset. Fortunately, as I delivered this message internally, I discovered that IBM was brimming with people who were not only ready to change, they were eager and able to make those changes.*

Jack Welch admits that GE could have been even more focused on the customer. In 1999, after learning that some customers were not feeling the effects of the Six Sigma initiative, he revised the GE values and implemented other tactics designed to ensure a more customer-oriented perspective. "Outside-in is a big idea," Welch argued. "We've been inside-out for over a hundred years. Forcing everything around the outside-in view will change the game."

Most of the leaders in this book were keenly aware that it was the customer who determined their company's fate, and so they spent significant portions of their time meeting with customers (in some cases upwards of 50 percent). Sam Walton put it very well when he said, "There is only one boss. The customer. And he can fire everybody in the company from the chairman on down, simply by spending his money somewhere else."

2. **MANY EXCEPTIONAL CEOS HAVE AN "EVANGELICAL LEADERSHIP GENE."** This particular trait should not be confused with what many people characterize as charisma. This is a critical point. Management theorist Peter Drucker feels that effective leadership has little to do with charisma. Drucker wrote, "Effective leadership doesn't depend on charisma. Dwight Eisenhower, George Marshall and Harry Truman were singularly effective leaders, yet none possessed more charisma than a dead mackerel." He adds that leadership is "mundane, unromantic and boring." Jim Collins, coauthor of the book *Built to Last* and *Good to Great*, agrees with Drucker's assessment, arguing that "a high-profile, charismatic style is absolutely not required to successfully shape a visionary company."

What's the difference between evangelism and charisma? The *American Heritage Dictionary* defines *evangelical* as "characterized by ardent or crusading enthusiasm; zealous."[2] The same dictionary defines *charisma* two ways. The first definition is "a rare personal quality attributed to leaders who arouse fervent popular devotion and enthusiasm." The second (or *b* definition) is "personal magnetism, or charm."

Drucker and Collins were invoking the "magnetism" definition when they argued that charisma is not required for effective leadership. And at the risk

[2] Religious definitions, which appear first in the entry, are excluded from this discussion.

of offending my subject CEOs, I don't think there is an overrepresentation of magnetic personalities in this book. On the other hand, the definition that speaks of arousing "popular devotion and enthusiasm" does seem to pertain. In fact, it's a most apt description of the seven leaders in this book.

My subject CEOs are secular evangelists. Without exception, they demonstrate an "ardent or crusading enthusiasm" for their jobs, their companies, and their causes. Each had a fire-in-the-belly excitement that helped to arouse enthusiasm in others. They felt strongly about a particular idea, product, or process, and were able to use the bully pulpit of their office effectively to spread their "gospel."

This evangelical trait has little to do with personal magnetism and everything to do with devotion or commitment to a cause or idea. Even a casual examination of the records of the seven leaders profiled in this book reveals evidence of their crusading traits. For example, Lou Gerstner didn't strike many people around him as the most magnetic of individuals, but he *did* display his evangelical trait when it came to shifting the company's mind-set. He was *intensely focused* on restoring an outside-in perspective. If you were around him for any period of time, you simply couldn't miss it.

When David Glass was asked whether "evangelical" was an apt description of the late Sam Walton, he answered unflinchingly, "He probably fits that description more than anyone else I know. That absolutely describes Sam." He added, "Strategically, you can make great decisions and that will not do a lot for you unless you have got that charismatic inspirational leader. And I have seen many businesses that are built on one or the other. You have to have both if you are ever going to have a great company. And that's what we happened to have at Wal-Mart."

It should be noted that Walton, like the majority of the CEOs profiled in this book, was the founder of his company. When Glass refers to building great businesses, he is referring to *starting* them. Once a company is established, particularly if it is a market leader, the importance of the founder's evangelism diminishes. As Glass stated, once the founder is gone, the company is able to follow his or her principles and philosophies, and to continue to build on them as the business expands. But when the company gets into trouble somewhere down the road—and it happens to almost every company sooner or later—evangelical leadership once again becomes important to the success of the organization.

Herb Kelleher was another CEO who could rightly be called a zealot, although his offbeat approach to leadership—which dates back to his earliest days at Southwest—sets him apart from other large-company executives. (The best-selling book written about him was affectionately entitled *Nuts*.) Like Wal-Mart's Sam Walton, however, Kelleher was deeply committed to fostering a community-like culture among both customers and employees. In early 2002, he offered the following advice:

Don't use the abstraction of "profit" as your goal in dealing with each other and the public. Instead, focus on great internal and external Customer Service so that the Customers will both rejoice and return, which is, of course, a key to profitability, most especially in difficult economic times.

He also wrote that Southwest "has many times sacrificed with respect to short-term profit levels in order to sustain the job security and livelihoods of our Employees."

Like all strong leaders, Kelleher practiced what he preached. Anyone who has ever taken a Southwest flight knows that it is a different experience from flying other commercial carriers. Jokes and good humor take the place of meals and assigned seating. Over the years, the airline has used some rather nontraditional methods to create a unique flying experience for its customers, and Kelleher has led the charge. He spent three decades making Southwest's culture one of its defining features, and he feels that it is one of the key assets of the company that cannot be duplicated.

Jack Welch had a different style from Walton and Kelleher, although he certainly shared their evangelical leanings. In particular, Welch displayed great enthusiasm for GE's growth initiatives. When describing why he would show such excitement over a companywide program like Six Sigma (the statistically based quality program he implemented in 1996), he replied, "One cannot be tentative" about things like this. One has to be on the "lunatic fringe," he asserted, adding that Six Sigma leaders are "changing the very DNA of GE culture."

So Welch was fiercely committed to Six Sigma, and the success of that initiative became part of his legacy. He never stopped communicating the message, and he used every weapon in his arsenal to convey it (everything from companywide emails to changing the list of GE's values to include the quality initiative). Like the other leaders in this book, Welch backed up his language with action. He made Six Sigma training mandatory for all professional-level employees, and he also made 40 percent of his senior managers' bonuses dependent upon the success of the program.

Welch had the ability to get hundreds of thousands of GE employees to fundamentally change the way they worked. Once he bought into a concept or initiative, he was able to use GE's operating system to spread it through all of GE's diverse businesses. And what sparked it all was Welch's commitment to an idea or program that he felt could strengthen GE's competitive position. His stated goal was to make GE the world's most competitive enterprise— an evangelical statement, certainly, designed to get others to commit to a particular driving passion.

Welch said that the best leaders are those who can articulate a vision and get others to execute it. His four Es of leadership, which he felt were the keys to effective leadership, were "energy," "energize," "edge," and "execute." Without an evangelical quality, it would be difficult to spark others to superior performance (energize). In Welch's Authentic Leadership Model, which was a precursor to the four Es, he includes the following success traits: "a good communicator," "a team builder," "energizes others," "has infectious enthusiasm," and "has fun doing it."

In the mid-1980s, as noted above, Andy Grove and his senior management team had to switch the entire focus of the company from memory chips to microprocessors. This was a monumental task. It would have been impossible to pull off without Grove's evangelical ability to convince others that he was leading them down the right path—even when he wasn't so sure himself. Says Grove, "You have to pretend you're 100% sure. You have to take action; you can't hesitate or hedge your bets. Anything less will condemn your actions to failure."

Each of the seven CEOs in this book had the benefit of an inner fire that was infectious. Each was able to set a strategic direction and use "ardent or crusading enthusiasm" to get people to work toward the company goals.

3. THE MOST EFFECTIVE BUSINESS LEADERS UNDERSTAND THE CRITICAL ROLE OF CULTURE, AND HOW DIFFICULT IT IS TO BRING ABOUT MEANINGFUL CULTURAL CHANGE. Authentic cultural change requires years, not months. Lou Gerstner called the process of transforming a culture "frustrating" and "mind-bendingly hard." Like the other managers in this book, he knew that his company's culture would be the key to enhancing performance and accomplishing key corporate goals. Gerstner succeeded in turning around IBM because he was able to transform the company's complacent

culture into one that was outwardly focused and far more competitive.

Andy Grove also felt that company culture was the key to maintaining a company's edge, but he had a unique approach. Having saved his company from several crises, he felt that it was important to maintain a culture in which employees were always on their guard. In fact, he argued that instilling fear in the ranks of the organization was a good thing. Only a culture that knew fear, argued Grove, could keep the organization out of the deadly trap of complacency.

By "instilling fear," of course, Grove did not mean fear of management or of colleagues; he meant fear of mortal external threats to the organization. "The most important role of managers is to create an environment in which people are passionately dedicated to winning in the marketplace," writes Grove. "Fear plays a major role in creating and maintaining such passion. Fear of competition, fear of bankruptcy, fear of being wrong and fear of losing all can be powerful motivators." Grove also claims that the only way to instill such a feeling in the rank and file is to lead by example—that is, by *feeling fear yourself.* Only then will the company be sufficiently inoculated against deadly organizational diseases.

As discussed earlier, Herb Kelleher felt that culture was the key to his company, but his approach was almost the opposite of Grove's. Kelleher thought it crucial that employees have fun on the job, and he fostered a culture that encouraged good humor. He believed that if he succeeded in this goal, his pilots and flight attendants would serve customers in much the same spirit. He even found ways to turn deadly serious disputes into light-hearted wrangles—like, for example, the time he turned a trademark dispute with another airline into an arm-wrestling contest between himself and his counterpart at the other company. Rather than generating rancor and huge legal bills, Kelleher further fueled the public perception that Southwest must be a hell of a fun place to work.

Jack Welch also understood the importance of culture, particularly after he made some of his most drastic restructuring moves in the mid-1980s. By the late 1980s, he had performed radical surgery on the company—a transformation unlike almost anything corporate America had ever seen. After downsizing GE by more than 100,000 workers and selling off more than 100 companies, he knew that he would have to restore the confidence of those who had survived the bloodletting. In 1989, therefore, he created Work-Out, a cultural initiative that gave the workers a say in how the businesses were run. That was Welch's key companywide cultural initiative, but it was a key step in building the learning culture that would become his trademark.

Michael Dell says, "Culture is one of those things where you know it when you see it, but it's a little bit hard to describe. Our culture is very results-oriented, very pragmatic. It stresses goals. . . . Now that we have the momentum of success, the reinforcement of that, it's kind of powerful." Michael Dell also described his culture as performance-oriented, suggesting that if you don't perform at Dell, you go someplace else. "Defensiveness is not something that works well within our culture," he adds. "We tend to be very self-critical, and we look for what we can fix and what we can improve, and we do it fast."

Wal-Mart's David Glass thinks that most managers don't fully grasp the importance of company culture: "I think it's way underestimated how important the culture has been to the company's success. . . . His [Walton's] philosophy in building the company that he built was, if you could make everyone a partner in the business, give them a voice in it, share the profits with them, make them an integral part of it, that worked a lot better than an employer/employee relationship. And that was sort of the basis for the Wal-Mart culture that got started."

To sum up: Although there were some major differences in how these seven leaders approached culture, they all knew how important a strong culture was to the company's success. Walton's and Kelleher's approaches were similar—that is, creating what might be called a more "family-oriented" culture. The others fostered a culture that was explicitly focused on "winning in the marketplace," as Grove put it. Of course, Walton and Kelleher wanted to win just as badly, but they thought that the key to their success would be found in their encouraging of a more nurturing, family-oriented environment.

4. **THESE CEOS CREATE OR ADAPT "NEXT-GENERATION" PRODUCTS, PROCESSES, OR SOLUTIONS.** This trait has a great deal to do with *vision*—the ability to anticipate emerging and future needs and to create products,

services, and new technologies capable of satisfying those needs. Sam Walton, in describing his years as a football player, admitted that he "had a good sense for where the ball was going to be." That seems like an apt description of how he and the other six leaders in this book approached their careers and their industries. All of them predicted the future of their industries accurately enough to produce products and businesses that could capitalize on their vision of the future. Few were perfect, but it is not necessary to spot every trend or to create products for every emerging technology. The key is to have *just enough prescience*—and also, of course, to create an organization capable of moving quickly if that vision does indeed become a reality.

In several cases, great companies were created because the founder identified an important trend and simply refused to let other companies beat his organization to the "vision." He saw something that portended the future of an industry, and he did not want it to happen without him.

This is particularly true of the leaders of technology-based companies, and four of the leaders in this book led such companies: Dell, IBM, Microsoft, and Intel. When it comes to creating technologies, a first-mover advantage (or at least an early-mover advantage) often spells the difference between success and failure.

Bill Gates recognized this more than a quarter century ago. Gates (and Microsoft cofounder Paul Allen) saw the future in 1975. Once the personal computer appeared on the horizon, Gates and Allen realized that software, not hardware, was the future. (In fact, it was seeing an advertisement for the new machine that panicked Gates: *Here was the future; how was he going to be part of it?*) The new device had an Intel 8080 microprocessor chip, which acted as its brain, but without software, it couldn't actually *do* very much. In *The Road Ahead*, Gates wrote of his response to seeing that advertisement for the Altair 8800:

> *Oh no, it's happening without us! People are going to write real software for this chip. I was sure it would happen sooner rather than later, and I wanted to be involved from the beginning. The chance to get in on the first stages of the PC revolution seemed the opportunity of a lifetime, and I seized it.*

Andy Grove was obviously a first mover in the microprocessor market, since his company had produced the chip that served as the brain of the Altair 8800. While Gates is correctly perceived as one of the architects of the computer revolution, Intel was founded seven years before Microsoft. Grove wrote that all start-ups are built around a core idea. The idea that sparked the creation of Intel was to produce a chip that would become the source of memory in computers. Although the first chip was primitive by today's standards (it was able to store only 64 data points, in contrast to the many millions of numbers stored by today's chips), it was nevertheless the beginning of a revolution.

Sam Walton saw the future of retailing in 1962, and it led him to shift his focus to that of a discounter. Discounting had been around in some form or another for years, and in 1962 it was already a $2 billion business. Walton was already a successful retailer, but he understood that he had to change his model or risk being put out of business.

Before creating Wal-Mart, Walton had a store named Walton's Family Center in St. Robert, Missouri, a town with a population of only 1500. The success of that store gave Walton a key piece of competitive information that would prove to be the deciding factor in launching Wal-Mart. His first deep-discount store—in Rogers, Arkansas—has been described as less like a business and more like a rummage sale. But it didn't matter that his stores were not yet as good as his competitors'; the key was that Walton had spotted the future of discounting and remade it in his own vision.

To be sure, his company benefited greatly from the economy and demographics of post–World War II America. But Wal-Mart would never have become so dominant if Walton had not looked into the future and improved on the retailing formula. His brother Bud once said that Sam "never stopped trying to do something different."

Jack Welch saw GE's future in the 1980s, and he knew that it would require a major overhaul of the company. He saw little growth in manufacturing, although that was what had defined the company since its founding by Thomas Edison a century earlier. To create the company he envisioned, Welch turned to technology and services. His decision to sell off GE's Housewares Division, which he felt did not fit his vision for GE, provoked fury among his critics, who considered the venerable division to be sacrosanct. In response to his detractors, he posed a question that not only gave them pause, but helped clarify his vision of the future: "In the twenty-first century, would you rather be in toasters or CT scanners?"

Welch also proved that adapting a process could catapult a company's culture and productivity to the next level. In 1996, he launched Six Sigma, the quality program pioneered in the United States by Motorola. Although he was the first to admit that GE did not create the program (in fact, Welch was late to the game and required some convincing from former GE vice chairman Larry Bossidy), he implemented the quality program with such vigor and comprehensiveness that he made it his own. It became the largest corporate initiative ever implemented at any company. It helped save the firm billions of dollars, while enhancing the quality of GE's products and services. (It also probably played a role in GE's selection of Jeff Immelt as Welch's successor, given that Immelt was a huge proponent of the program.)

When he took the reins at IBM, Lou Gerstner did not know all that much about computers, but he knew that IBM would "have to stop standing on the wrong side of history" if the company was to survive. Gerstner said that the company had to decide

where the industry was going to be 5 or 10 years down the road, [and then] build the company that was going to have a shot at leading the industry again based on this series of fundamental decisions. What matters now is the integration of all the pieces with each other, the integration of technology with business processes, and the integration of all these formerly self-standing processes with one another.

Along with the six other CEOs profiled in this volume, Gerstner realized that building (or turning around) a successful firm depended on looking past the present and deducing where the company's future market was likely to reside. All seven calculated correctly, and in each case, their stakeholders were rewarded.

5. **THESE LEADERS IMPLEMENTED THE *BEST IDEAS*, REGARDLESS OF THEIR ORIGIN.** This is a hallmark of exceptional leaders, and also a key characteristic of a learning culture. In a learning organization, leaders encourage their managers and employees to glean the best ideas from any source. At least two of the companies profiled in this book—IBM and GE—had run into trouble when their managers stopped searching outside the company for answers, feeling that they already had all the answers.

Sam Walton's singular obsession with finding the best ideas has already been discussed at length. Of all of the leaders in this book, none was more obsessive about learning from competitors than Walton. Even before he opened his first Wal-Mart, Walton had gotten into the habit of studying other stores. According to his wife, Helen, Walton spent as much time in his rivals' stores as in his own. And he once confessed that almost everything he tried in his stores he had copied from someone else.

Although he didn't open his first Wal-Mart until 1962, by 1960 Walton had already made trips to the East Coast to examine E. J. Korvette stores (an early discounter) and to meet with the heads of such discounting pioneers as Spartans, Zayre, and Mammoth Mart. He said that a lesson that had stuck with him throughout his life was that you can learn from anyone, particularly the competitor across the street. In that spirit, he absorbed good ideas, and improved on them.

Jack Welch later institutionalized that behavior, setting up formal processes to gather, analyze, and act upon good ideas. He declared that learning from competitors not only was fair, but was the job of every GE employee.

Welch made *learning* and *ideas* the centerpiece of GE's culture, and he became intensely focused on spreading good thinking around the company. Over the years, he was more than happy to give credit to other companies that GE had learned from. Lessons gleaned from IBM and Johnson & Johnson, he said, helped the company get a foothold in the Chinese market. He said that it was Canon and Chrysler that had taught GE some of its product-launching techniques. Some leaders like to believe—or would like *you* to believe—that they thought of everything themselves. Leaders like Walton and Welch couldn't have cared less about whose idea it was. They cared about how quickly, and how effectively, that idea got embraced.

6. **EXCEPTIONAL CEOS ADVANCE THE LEADERSHIP BODY OF KNOWLEDGE IN SOME MEANINGFUL FASHION.** There are legions of accomplished CEOs who live up to the

aforementioned criteria, but who still do not appear in this book. I omitted many of those individuals because there is no strong evidence that they advanced management thinking in any significant way.

Each of the seven CEOs who *are* profiled in this book rewrote an important aspect of the leadership playbook. Bill Gates, the coiner of the phrase "digital nervous system," put information on the desktop and devised revolutionary ways for companies to move that information around the organization and thereby make *all* employees knowledge workers. Andy Grove wrote extensively about "strategic inflection points," a concept that helped managers better understand the complexities of dealing with radical change.

Herb Kelleher taught managers that company culture can become one of an organization's great assets, and that work can indeed be about more than numbers and boredom and punching clocks. He inculcated spirit and good humor into the fabric of Southwest Airlines, making it a habit to remember the birthdays and anniversaries of his employees. They rewarded him and the company for it by going the extra mile for the organization. When asked what was the difference that made Southwest a profitable airline for three straight decades, he would answer unhesitatingly: his people.

The same could be said for Sam Walton, who was surprised that other people were surprised that he drove around in a pick-up truck. ("What am I supposed to drive my dogs around in," he once asked, "a Rolls Royce?") As mentioned previously, his love for learning is something that all managers could learn from. His adherence to a simple yet immensely powerful vision (i.e., everyday lowest prices) carries with it a profound message for the Sam Waltons of future generations.

When it came to rewriting the leadership rulebook, Jack Welch turned out to be in a class by himself. He said, "Business is simple," and he asserted that there was great power in informality. Up to that point, business had been anything but informal. He created a meritocracy in which the best ("A" players) excelled and thrived. He saw that business is all about building the *intellect* of the organization—a profound thought, coming from a chief executive. He created certain measurements that would become benchmarks for other corporations around the world, such as double-digit growth and becoming "number one or number two" in all markets. But it was his creation of an effective, coherent learning organization out of a collection of so many disparate businesses that is likely to stand as his major achievement.

A final word on what made these leaders tick—or, more precisely, on what *didn't* make them tick: As reported earlier in this chapter, Peter Drucker once declared leadership to be "mundane, unromantic, and boring." I think that every one of the seven leaders in this book would disagree with Drucker on this point. Sam Walton called building Wal-Mart fun and exciting, and wrote of his passion to compete. In a similar vein, Jack Welch once declared, "Business is ideas and fun and excitement and celebrations, all those things." But perhaps the leader who summed it up best was Michael Dell. In 1999, he was speaking to an entrepre-

The Traits/Accomplishments of Exceptional Leaders

1. An "outside-in" perspective

2. An evangelical leadership gene

3. Understands the critical role of culture

4. Creates next generation products, processes, or solutions

5. Implements the best ideas, regardless of origin

6. Advances the leadership body of knowledge

neurship class at his alma mater, the University of Texas, when a student asked why the multibillionaire continued to work. "You've got so much money," the bold young student declared. "Why don't you just sell out, buy a boat, and sail off to the Caribbean?"

Dell's answer said it all: "Sailing's boring. Do you have any idea how much *fun* it is to run a billion-dollar company?"

What follows are the leadership lessons of seven exceptional leaders who changed the face of business and had a great deal of fun along the way.

PART 2

Defining Strategies of Exceptional Leaders

CHAPTER 2

Place the Customer at the Epicenter of the Business Model

———————

From the start, our entire business—from design to manufacturing to sales—was oriented around listening to the customer.
—MICHAEL DELL, founder & CEO, Dell Computer

Being in touch with customer needs is . . . always important. But perhaps more important when needs are changing—and generally that occurs during an economic downturn—you want to understand those better than any other company.

—MICHAEL DELL

What Would Michael Dell Do?

In the seat of the CEO: You are the CEO of a $30 million company that produces consumer products for the home. The company, founded by your father in the 1960s, was a pioneer in producing air-purifying products for home use. Two years ago your father retired, turning the business over to you. Your first moves involved modernizing the company by installing a state-of-the-art computer system (including a company web site) for both backroom operations and order procurement. As a result, today more than half the company's orders are processed via the Internet.

All went smoothly for the first 6 months. After that, though, things went downhill. Although the company's first products were air humidifiers and dehumidifiers, the firm's number one product for the past 4 years has been an air-purifier (the AirPure 4000). When the company first introduced the product, it was an instant hit. But new competitors have entered the market and are practically destroying you. If things continue at this pace, within 6 months you will have less than a quarter of the market share you enjoyed only a year ago. To make matters worse, you have a growing inventory problem, since demand has fallen so dramatically. If things don't turn around, you will have to write off more than a million dollars in excess inventory.

Since the product has not changed, you cannot understand what is going on. To counter the new competition, you followed your father's advice and launched a new marketing campaign. This effort included dozens of print and radio advertisements, as well as a huge promotional mailing of fliers offering unbelievable discounts. Already, the verdict on that campaign is clear: The new advertising and direct-mail campaigns were expensive, and they didn't work.

You're stumped. Your product is priced competitively and gets high grades on quality surveys. It even comes with a 100 percent guarantee. What do you do now? Is there any way to turn things around? What moves might you make to stop the plunge in market share of your number one product?

What would Michael Dell do?

When Michael Dell was 12, he issued his first product catalog. It was called "Dell's Stamps," and he advertised it in a local trade journal. By going directly to the ultimate user, the young entrepreneur learned his first lesson about developing a direct relationship with the customer.

After spending a good part of his high school years fiddling with computers and hanging out at the local Radio Shack, Dell—like lots of other 19-year-olds—went off to college. But that's where his life stopped following the common path. Within months, Dell had turned his dorm room into a personal-computer laboratory. Before long, he was selling personal computers. In 1984, he made it official, registering his business as Dell Computer Corporation.

Just 4 years later, the company went public, raising $30 million in its initial public offering. At age 27, Michael Dell was the youngest CEO of a *Fortune* 500 company. Dell Computer Corporation emerged as a true phenomenon. It was the number one stock of the 1990s, soaring almost 90,000 percent. According to Michael Dell, the key to his company's success was the customer:

From the start, our entire business—from design to manufacturing to sales—was oriented around listening to the customer, responding to the customer, and delivering what the customer wanted.

While Dell's words sound almost like platitudes in today's competitive world, at that time building an entire business by placing the customer at the epicenter was anything but common. Dell's direct model is based on a one-to-one relationship between the company and the customer—there are no intermediaries, no middlemen. (On one occasion, Dell experimented with an indirect model—a product sold through computer stores—but the effort failed, and Dell vowed never again to waver from the company's original vision.) This was a case of philosophy converging with necessity:

We started the company by building to the customer's order. And interestingly enough, we didn't do it because we saw some massive paradigm in the future. Basically, we just didn't have any capital [to mass-produce].

Like other great success stories, Dell's direct model of "mass customization" was not born of any desire to revolutionize an industry. Instead, it was forged through a "bottom-up" strategy based on customers' needs and preferences. The lesson is clear: Managers hoping to create successful brands cannot do it by imposing their own views (or, worse, the management committee's views!) on the marketplace. Somehow, someway, there needs to be a mechanism in place whereby the company learns to make the products that its target customers actually want.

Dell says that while other companies *guess* what their customers want, his company *knows*. Through hundreds of thousands of calls, emails, and faxes from customers, the company gets vital information about the features that people will pay for in a computer and what capabilities they might be looking for (and, again, paying for) in the future. And this information is closely tied to the company's manufacturing strategy: Unlike its competitors, Dell does not even build the product until *after* the order comes in. In addition to heading off inventory backlogs and cash flow problems, this method has the advantage of ensuring that customers' needs are met *precisely*. In the mercilessly competitive computer industry, that knowledge advantage affords the company a decisive edge:

> *As a natural extension of customer contact, the direct model allows us to take the pulse of whatever market we move into and provide the right technology for the right customers. The direct model has become the backbone of our company and the greatest tool in its growth. It all evolved from the basic idea of eliminating the middleman.*

With no middleman intervening, the company is able to get a constant flow of unfiltered information from its customer base. The lesson of the direct model is clear: To duplicate Dell's success, other companies must find ways to develop a relationship with the end users of their product, even if their business models do not resemble Dell's.

Here are three things that managers can do to cultivate

closer relationships with end users while also garnering key information and product feedback:

- SPEND MORE TIME WITH CUSTOMERS. Whether you are a CEO, a director of sales, or an account manager, there is simply no substitute for frequent face-to-face meetings with customers. Many top CEOs report that they spend upwards of 50 percent of their time with customers, and they add that this is often the most important part of their day.

- INVITE KEY CUSTOMERS IN TO SPEAK TO KEY UNITS. An alternative to visiting customers is having customers visit you. Create a forum where they can speak with your key people, either publicly or in smaller groups. This will not only provide key information and insights, but also send an important message to those customers.

- USE THE INTERNET AND OTHER NONINTERMEDIATED MEANS TO CREATE AN ONGOING CUSTOMER RELATIONSHIP. While technology should not be used as the sole means of staying in contact with customers, sending email "blasts" to customers informing them of new product updates, etc., can be effective. Make sure, however, that the communication is not strictly one-way. Getting customers' feedback is a crucial step in the process.

Delivering exactly what the customer wants is one of the ingredients of Dell's success. Price is the other. Dell became successful not only by fulfilling customer needs with high-quality products, but also by doing so at rock-bottom prices. With no distributors requiring their own margin, Dell is able to pass substantial savings on to its customers:

We're in the business of dramatically reducing the cost of distributing technology. To do that, we are going to get closer and closer to our suppliers and our customers.

This is an important lesson for companies that operate in ultra-competitive, price-sensitive markets. Whenever such an organization achieves some meaningful cost advantage, it does best when it passes at least a significant percentage of those savings on to consumers. This does not mean that a company should not maintain healthy profit margins, but squeezing every penny of profit out of a transaction may ultimately lead an otherwise healthy company to falter.

ACCELERATING MARKET SHARE IN *BAD* TIMES

One test of a corporate strategy is to see how well it performs in bad times. By that measure, Dell's direct distribution model has proved itself to be a solid success. In the recession that gripped the computer industry in the early 2000s, Dell continued to grow at a healthy rate. Despite industry retrenchment and consolidation, Dell continued to enjoy—in Michael Dell's phrase—"hefty profits." Why?

It goes back to the structural cost advantage, which is very much at the root of our business model in terms of having a more efficient distribution. Eliminating dealers, middlemen, inventories; the Internet; all the efficiencies that we have been working so hard to drive have kind of kicked in the afterburners in the last 12 months.

Additional evidence that this was a successful strategy is not hard to find. During the technology bust of 2001, for example, Dell cut the prices of its computers. This prompted at least one competitor to criticize Dell for allegedly igniting a price war, which this competitor described as a "dumb" move. Michael Dell shrugged off the salvo, responding, "If you don't have the real ability to differentiate, a price war is dumb." According to Dell, that was exactly the position his competitor was in— and it was no surprise, he added, that his rival was in the process of making a "very substantial exit" from that market.

Nor did Michael Dell express much concern about "the most rapid market consolidation ever" in his relatively young industry. Rather than threatening Dell's competitive position, all that consolidation and market churning actually *enhanced* Dell's competitive position:

Essentially we have now taken on the number one share position on a worldwide basis. We have seen about a seven-point swing in market share in the United States on a year-by-year basis. So officially [rapid market consolidation] has accelerated in about four quarters what it normally has taken us about nine or ten quarters to do, in terms of a shift in market share.

When consumers—companies and individuals alike— begin tightening their belts, the odds go up that the best product at the best price will win the day. So the company's countercyclical increase in market share during hard times grew directly out of its ability to gauge demand, produce a superior product, and ultimately deliver better value than its rivals.

The real takeaway from this episode is probably self-evident. The pieces of the puzzle have to fit together in a mutually reinforcing way. Unless your firm is able to achieve genuine differentiation—through quality of product, a better price, superior service, ease of use, etc.—then price wars alone are unlikely to address your firm's competitive woes. On the other hand, if you are able to truly differentiate your product or service and then deliver it at a lower (and profitable) price, you can sustain a genuine competitive advantage.

THE "DEMAND SIDE" OF THE DELL STRATEGY

Obviously, the direct model is an unusual approach to distribution that wouldn't meet the needs of most businesses. Still, other organizations can incorporate vital elements of Dell's model into their own operations. For example, Dell stresses that during tough economic times, it is especially important to understand and anticipate customer demand—a crucial element of Dell's strategic advantage. The problem, says Dell, is that most companies don't really know how to accurately forecast demand:

> First, if you just step back from whether it's direct or indirect and you just look at the way business works . . . it's based on the assumption that you don't really know when and how the demand is going to occur.

Although gauging customer demand became somewhat easier for some companies once Internet technology transformed assumptions and business models, it continues to be a difficult undertaking for most companies. Again, the evidence abounds: If forecasting demand were easy, the business news would include far fewer stories of excess inventory and multibillion-dollar write-offs.[1]

Nimbleness is a critical ingredient. Dell says it is imperative that companies "be prepared for all possible . . . instances of demand whenever and wherever they may occur." Of course, that's relatively easy for a company like Dell, with its "made to order" mentality and model. But Michael Dell argues that, to a large extent, the key to enhancing productivity and profitability for companies without a direct model is the correct use of technology, and in particular, the Internet.

He admits that the Internet was tailor-made for his company, allowing the firm to gauge demand more accurately than ever before. In early 2002, Dell was raking in between $60 and $70 million of sales over the Internet on a *daily* basis, and Dell is hoping to boost this number substantially within a couple of years. Again, the way he plans to get there has implications for many kinds of businesses:

> *There are goals to have 100 percent of our sales on line . . . that's the only correct goal for us as far as we're concerned . . . so we keep*

---

[1] The great NASDAQ meltdown of 2000–2002 occurred in part because companies built up excessive inventories on the assumption that the voracious demand for technology of the late 1990s would continue into the new century. When demand failed to materialize, companies missed earnings and sales targets by wide margins, and hundreds of billions of dollars disappeared from the stock market as the vast majority of technology stocks plummeted. Dell was not immune; its market capitalization also dropped. In essence, the market reevaluated the true worth of all technology stocks. This took the air out of the NASDAQ bubble, which was caused, in large part, by the exaggerated valuation of Internet stocks.

driving in that direction. . . . Evolution follows a couple of different
paths. One is machine-to-machine communication.

Another part of the formula is *automation*, especially in
the order process. The goal is to get machines talking to
machines. A machine at a client company places an order
with a machine at Dell. That triggers the entire made-to-
order process, which then becomes more or less automatic.
"Over 90 percent of our supply-chain transactions are
machine-to-machine transactions," Dell says with obvious
satisfaction. Of course, "you have to put some sort of
human framework in there. But if all transactions were
non-Internet individual purchases [that is, individual orders placed over the phone], the expense would be just
enormous."

Based on Michael Dell's experience, there are several
things that any organization should keep in mind in order
to maximize sales opportunities and keep costs down:

- FIND BETTER WAYS TO GAUGE DEMAND. The basis of the
  Dell model is an incredibly firm grasp on demand.
  Other companies, regardless of their size, can help
  their own cause by doing a better job of forecasting
  demand and, in Michael Dell's words, being "prepared for all possible instances of demand, whenever
  and wherever they may occur."

- MOVE AS MUCH BUSINESS AS POSSIBLE ONTO THE INTER-
  NET, AND INCREASE THE PERCENTAGE OF "MACHINE-TO-
  MACHINE" BUSINESS. Dell may never reach his goal of
  garnering 100 percent of his sales online. But remember that 90 percent of his supply-chain transactions are

machine-to-machine. This may be unrealistic for many companies, but moving in this direction can lower transaction costs, while freeing up employees to get more involved with knowledge-based activities that can help the company in other ways.

INVOLVE CUSTOMERS *FIRST* TO AVOID DISASTERS

Even great companies make mistakes, and Michael Dell admits that his company is no exception. In 1989, Dell introduced a new family of products, code-named Olympic. Olympic was a line of desktop and workstation computers that were able to perform a wide array of tasks. The product introduction—Dell's biggest ever—turned out to be the company's biggest-ever flop. While the products were impressive from a technology standpoint, customers just didn't *need* such complex products with that much technological firepower. The failure of Olympic delivered a powerful lesson to the relatively young company, and it was one that Michael Dell would not soon forget:

We had gone ahead and created a product that was, for all intents and purposes, technology for technology's sake, rather than technology for the customer's sake. If we had consulted our customers first about what they needed . . . we could have saved ourselves a lot of aggravation.

Michael Dell urges all companies to involve their customers earlier in the process. He feels that failed products are often the result of companies' launching new products without sufficient knowledge of their customers. He believes that it is incumbent upon organizations to provide useful information up and down the supply chain. He warns that companies that ignore this advice do so at their own peril:

> *If your business isn't enabled by customers and suppliers having more information and being able to use it, you're probably already in trouble. The Internet is like a weapon sitting on a table ready to be picked up by either you or your competitors.*

INVOLVE *EVERYONE* IN CREATING
VALUE FOR THE CUSTOMER

The company obviously gleaned important lessons from its mistake. After Olympic, Dell started talking about "relevant technology," meaning only those technologies that are important to its customers. But Olympic also taught Michael Dell that just about everyone needs to be involved in serving customers—even engineers and technicians. It would have been easy to blame Olympic on the engineers, but Michael Dell felt that it wasn't their fault. Why? Because, for structural reasons, *they didn't know the company's customers.* What to do? The company began to encourage its engineers to spend more time with sales teams and get more involved in product planning. While some resisted, many welcomed the chance to play a more prominent role in the entire process:

> *Teaching bright technical people to think beyond the technology and in terms of what people really want—and what makes for good*

business—isn't always easy. It can take time, but it can best be done by immersing them in the buying process and involving them in the strategy and logic that go in deciding what creates value for customers.

The lessons Michael Dell learned from the failure of Olympic are relevant to the vast majority of organizations, and are worth noting here:

- ORGANIZATIONS AND PRODUCT MANAGERS CANNOT, AND SHOULD NOT, IMPOSE THEIR VIEWS ON THE MARKET-PLACE. Don't assume that just because you make a product—even one that you and your co-managers believe is spectacular—it will sell. Customers will always have the final say, and customers have a way of surprising you.

- INVOLVE CUSTOMERS AS EARLY IN THE PROCESS AS POSSI-BLE. If you ignore customers during the product-development process, you do so at your own peril. Involve customers as early as possible—and then *keep* them involved in the process.

- GET AS MANY PEOPLE AS POSSIBLE INSIDE THE COMPANY INVOLVED IN SATISFYING CUSTOMERS. Silos in organizations tend to develop over time. Functional areas like R&D and engineering tend to get insulated and isolated over time. The challenge for management is to involve as many individuals and departments as possible in determining the preferences and needs of core customers.

STRUCTURE THE ORGANIZATION AROUND
THE CUSTOMER (HOW DELL ACTS SMALL
WHILE GETTING BIGGER)

In the late 1990s, Michael Dell took customer focus one step further by *structuring the organization around the customer.* He had become convinced that organizing by product alone would not ensure the high-quality customer relationships he hoped to achieve. (If the company organizes only by product, says Dell, there is an assumption that the leaders of those divisions know everything about their target customers—not only domestically, but also around the globe.) Instead, he decided to segment by *both* product and customer. This way, product teams would have the information they need in order to satisfy specific customer segments.

First, Dell created several distinct sales organizations, each focused on serving the needs of a particular customer segment. As the company got bigger, he split the segments even further:

- Large and medium-sized companies

- Educational and government organizations

- Small businesses and consumers

This degree of segmentation not only reinforces Dell's commitment to satisfying customer's needs, but also ensures that the accountability for satisfying customers is shared throughout Dell's ranks. But Dell didn't stop there.

He further extended the customer segmentation model, creating complete business units organized around different customer types, each with its own sales, service, finance, IT, technical support, and manufacturing pieces. He credits the company's segmentation with supporting and reinforcing the direct approach:

Segmentation takes the closed feedback loop and makes it even smaller and more intimate. It refines our relationship with our customers.

As the company has grown, it has spun off some of these groups focused on customer segments into de facto small companies, each with its own organization team. That model enables Dell—today a huge company by almost any measure—to act with the spirit and responsiveness of dozens of small companies. Without a doubt, it gives Dell a decided edge in the marketplace.

What can other companies learn from the way Dell is organized? Here are some ideas that can prove useful in almost any organization:

- ORGANIZE AROUND THE CUSTOMER. The key is to get as many people in your organization as possible involved in satisfying the customer. Review the organizational chart with a fresh eye, and determine whether the way you are organized achieves this important goal.

- IF POSSIBLE, SEGMENT THE FIRM BY BOTH PRODUCT AND CUSTOMER, OR CREATE CROSS-FUNCTIONAL TEAMS THAT CAN DO SO. The key is to make sure that as many people in your organization as possible *know the customers*—their needs, desires, preferences, and so on.

If you can't organize the company in that manner for some reason, consider creating ad hoc cross-functional teams or task forces designed around specific customer groups or clusters.

- **GET YOUR COMPANY TO MOVE WITH THE RESPONSIVENESS OF A SMALL COMPANY.** Most large companies eventually get mired in bureaucracy, and when they do, it is the customer who suffers. One key to winning in the marketplace is to make sure that your firm is streamlined in a way that does not penalize the customer for your mistakes. In other words, get the people in your organization to adopt a small-company mind-set. Get them to move faster, respond more quickly, and anticipate customer needs more effectively. Get them to be more proactive, so that they won't have to play catch-up later.

Don't Forget about *Potential* Customers

Peter Drucker, the ageless management author, makes a critical point about customers that is worth repeating here. He urges companies not to forget about the customers who don't currently use their products—in other words, those who have the *potential* to become customers. After all, says Drucker, even the best companies don't have a lock on the whole market, and far too many companies forget about this crucial constituency.

As an example of what can go wrong when a business forgets about potential customers, Drucker cites a case far removed from Dell's world of computers—the fall of the big-city department stores:

Marketing starts with all customers in the market rather than with our customers. Even a powerful business rarely has a market share much larger than 30 percent. This means that 70 percent of the customers buy from someone else. Yet most businesses or industries pay no more attention to this 70 percent than the department stores did.

Drucker implores managers to pay attention to the inherent changes in demography that may transform the markets in which their business operates. These changes should be viewed not as threats, but as sources of new business, for the shifting environment changes the customer landscape of many businesses. He also points out that customers define markets, and that potential customers offer organizations the best opportunities with the least amount of risk. But market knowledge can go only so far in helping a business to snare new customers. It is not knowledge, cautions Drucker, but *actions* that will ultimately determine a company's success.

What Would Michael Dell Do?

Let's return now to the scenario at the beginning of the chapter—in which, you'll recall, you are the CEO of a $30 million consumer-products manufacturer that has fallen on hard times. I hope that, based on a review of how Michael Dell has built his company, the answer to the question posed is reasonably obvious.

First, you'll have to agree that it is unlikely that Michael Dell would have gotten into such a jam. Why? Because once the company's web site was constructed—remember, you launched it shortly after taking over—he would have used the site to garner as much information as possible from his customers.

Your major problem is that you don't know *why* your number one product is hemorrhaging market share. Let's back up 18 months, to when the AirPure 4000 started to lose market share. Faced with that situation, Michael Dell would have used all means possible to find out why. He would probably have arranged for a customer questionnaire to be prominently featured on the web site (perhaps rewarding respondents with cash-off coupons). Had he done so, he most likely would have discovered the key to the entire problem: The AirPure 4000 was not designed to clean mold spores from the air! During the last 2 years, air allergens and mold spores have become your customers' chief concern, but you had no idea about this. Your top competitor has been taking away your core customers by featuring this product benefit.

Next, he would have found a way to hold off producing the product until the order came in. Obviously, this would have prevented the inventory backlog that is adding to the company's red ink. Perhaps he would have found a way to let customers choose the features that were most important to them. For example, perhaps some buyers of the AirPure 4000 were interested only in cleaning pet dander from the air, while others were interested in eliminating smoke.

And finally, he would have worked to increase the percentage of sales that come in via the Internet. Remember, Michael Dell's own goal is to secure 100 percent of the company's sales from the Web. (Those sales save the company money!) Right now, you are at 50 percent—not bad by most measures, but probably a long way from where you could be if you offered additional incentives for buyers.

ASSESSING YOUR CEO QUOTIENT

1. How effectively has your organization incorporated the needs and desires of your customers into the everyday running of your business?

2. How often do senior managers of your company meet with customers?

3. Do you feel that your organization gets sufficient feedback directly from your customers? How could you learn more about your customers' specific needs and desires as they relate to your product or service?

4. Is your organization's product-development model built around the customer? If not, think about how you can involve the customer earlier on in the development model.

5. What does your organization do to ensure that the technical teams (e.g., engineers, scientists, computer scientists) better understand the needs of the customers? Do they participate in the product-development process?

6. Has not involving the customer in your strategic planning and/or product development led to product failures? Could those blunders been avoided?

7. What are you doing to learn more about potential customers? How can increased customer knowledge turn potential customers into actual customers?

MORE LESSONS FROM THE CEO

The Dell direct model is a complex business model that is obviously difficult to duplicate. Still, there are many ways in which your company can become more customer-focused. Here are a few ideas.

1. MAKE A COMMITMENT TO LEARN MORE ABOUT YOUR CUSTOMERS. Meet with key customers as often as it makes sense to do so, and make sure that all the people in your division do the same. Incorporate this sort of behavior into the regular culture of the business.

2. WHEN MEETING WITH CUSTOMERS, MAKE SURE TO USE THE TIME WISELY BY GETTING SPECIFIC FEEDBACK ABOUT THEIR NEEDS, PREFERENCES, ETC. Prepare for the meeting ahead of time by writing a short list of questions. (Remember: Customers will appreciate your interest, and they will appreciate it even more if you respect their time.)

3. IF YOUR COMPANY DOESN'T ALREADY DO SO, PLAN ON CONDUCTING AT LEAST ONE CUSTOMER SURVEY EACH YEAR IN AN AREA THAT WOULD BENEFIT FROM IN-CREASED CUSTOMER KNOWLEDGE. Once the results are in, make sure that you use the information by incorporating this feedback into the appropriate parts of the company. If your company uses the Internet to elicit company feedback, and if you're confident that this approach paints a reasonably accurate picture, then an annual survey may not be necessary.

4. KEEPING THE DELL MODEL IN MIND, TARGET AREAS THAT WOULD MOST BENEFIT FROM INCREASED CUS-TOMER INVOLVEMENT. Some examples are strategic planning, product development, and promotional planning. Focus on key products, key customer groups, and so on. Also, keeping Drucker's ideas in mind, you may want to devote resources to potential customers and customer groups in order to increase your market share in new areas.

5. ONCE YOU DECIDE WHICH AREAS YOU WANT TO FOCUS ON, WRITE A BRIEF PLAN INCORPORATING YOUR IDEAS FOR INCREASING CUSTOMER INVOLVEMENT. Share it with your manager and appropriate colleagues, and secure their commitment to executing the plan within a specified time frame.

CHAPTER 3

Create an Authentic Learning Organization

Our behavior is driven by a fundamental core belief: the desire, and the ability, of an organization to continuously learn from any source, anywhere; and to rapidly convert this learning into action is its ultimate competitive advantage.

—JACK WELCH, former CEO of General Electric

This boundaryless learning culture killed any view that assumed the "GE way" was the only way or even the best way. The operative assumption today is that someone, somewhere, has a better idea; and the operative compulsion is to find out who has that better idea, learn it, and put it into action—fast.

—JACK WELCH

What Would Jack Welch Do?

In the seat of the CEO: You are the CEO of a $25 billion conglomerate founded more than a century ago. Although you spent 20 years working your way up through the hierarchy, you were still surprised at the extent of the bureaucracy you discovered once you reached the corner office. Even though your company is heralded the world over for its excellence in management, you see a company that is hamstrung by red tape—an organization that seems to require seven signatures for every major decision.

After reviewing the organizational charts, you focus on a possible cause of all of this red tape: layer upon layer of management. There are more than 25,000 managers in the firm, including more than 130 vice presidents. There are so many strategic planners mucking up the works that nothing seems to get done. There are vice presidents hiring strategic planners, and strategic planners hiring vice presidents. On top of that, many of the company's largest businesses, such as its large tool division, are growing at less than 4 percent a year. No wonder the company has been dubbed a "GNP company"—its profits are growing at approximately the same rate as the economy as a whole.

And—you notice with concern—nobody seems to *mind*. You call a meeting with your senior management team to get its take on the situation, and you learn that most of its members are content with the way the company is functioning. They see little reason to change things. There is even a whiff of arrogance around the edges of the discussion—as if your colleagues are convinced that your company has a monopoly on good ideas and smart management.

This attitude is all the more surprising given the lack of coordination and communication that you've discovered among the members of this same management team. Despite the fact that most of them have been with the company for many years, they seem to know little about one another's businesses. In addition, when you ask them about the morale of the workforce, few seem to know (or perhaps care) how the rank and file are faring.

As if this weren't enough for you to worry about, many of the company's flagship businesses are lackluster at best. Rather than leading their industries, many of them are laggards (often fourth or fifth in their industries). You see few realistic growth prospects for these stragglers. Not surprisingly, the managers of these slow-growth companies have few strong ideas for improving things.

To complicate matters further, the company has its hand in so many types of businesses that you see no clear way to reorganize things. You see an organization in desperate need of an overhaul, and yet you seem to be alone in that assessment.

What is going on? Is your concern misplaced? If not, what do you do, and where do you begin?

What would Jack Welch do?

It was the publishing event of the year. When word spread in July of 2000 that the leadership memoirs of GE's Jack Welch were about to go on the auction block, every publisher wanted in. However, the multimillion-dollar ante was too much for most publishing houses. After several days of bidding, the price tag reached a stratospheric $7 million, and only two publishers were left standing. For a business book, this was an unheard-of event.

According to one insider, the GE chairman was embarrassed about the mountain of money that was about to be shoveled his way (despite the fact that he was planning to donate the money to charity). As a result, Welch put an end to the auction by selecting Time Warner, who agreed to pay $7.1 million for the right to publish his story. Had Welch not stopped the bidding, the price tag would probably have increased by several additional millions.

At that time, no U.S. president—traditionally the highest-paid autobiographers—had ever received a book advance of more than $7 million. (President Ronald Reagan had received $8 million, but this was for a two-book deal—his memoirs and a book of speeches). Why were the reflections of this business leader now more highly valued than the reminiscences of any other business or political leader in history?

Like the stock market, the Welch payday had reached record—even euphoric—levels. That same year, the greatest bull market in U.S. history ended. The following year, Welch stepped down as GE's CEO. Still, neither event prevented Welch's book from becoming one of the best-selling business books in publishing history. What made Jack Welch's leadership methods the most emulated in history? Why are his strategies and tactics studied by students, managers, and other chief executives the world over?

THE WELCH LEGACY

Jack Welch achieved extraordinary results with uncanny consistency. He achieved double-digit growth year after year, helping to build his reputation as an iconic business leader who could do no wrong. He was a role model for others to emulate: Double-digit annual growth became the benchmark for all CEOs and corporations in America. Welch debunked many of the most common myths of management—for example, that the command-and-control model is the best way to run a large company. But his ultimate legacy is that he created a learning culture within a mammoth corporation that had an amazingly diverse business portfolio.

Welch defined a learning organization as an organization in which employees and managers soak up good ideas from everywhere. He felt that the organizations that would ultimately achieve a sustainable competitive advantage were those that continuously learned, and then translated that learning into action. He observed frequently that it was a badge of honor to learn from someone else. "You need to believe that you are a learning institution," he once commented, "and to constantly challenge everything you have."

In a learning organization, employees are given access to critical information and are expected to search out creative solutions to problems. This model is the antithesis of Frederick W. Taylor's scientific management, a hierarchical system based on the notion that the primary function of workers is to perform specific routine tasks endlessly. Since the early years of the twentieth century, scientific management had been regarded as the most efficient way to get things done within a large corporation.

However, this assumes that managers know how to break a system down into its component parts and run that system most efficiently. At the heart of any learning culture, in contrast, is the assumption that the company and its managers *don't* have all the answers. Before Welch, relatively few GE managers saw good reason to look outside the company for better answers. Welch put an end to the "not invented here" arrogance. He felt that it was every employee's responsibility to seek out the best ideas, regardless of their origin. He proclaimed:

The hero is the one with the ideas.

At GE, said Welch, it was not the "stripes on one's shoulder" that determined someone's worth to the company, but the quality of one's ideas. For example, during a trip to the United Kingdom in 1999, a GE manager told Welch about a "reverse mentoring" program in which the youngest people in the organization taught the oldest how to use the Internet. "It was the best idea I ever heard," said Welch, who implemented the idea with his top 1000 managers within 2 weeks.

The GE chairman made sure that he practiced what he preached, getting a mentor of his own. "We celebrate ideas," he later said, referring to his budding computer literacy. "We put them online."

To begin to inculcate this learning mind-set into your own organization, try implementing the following:

- **LEAD BY EXAMPLE BY IMPORTING THE BEST IDEAS INTO YOUR ORGANIZATION.** Never stop scanning the marketplace and the competitive environment to get new ideas. Consider inviting leaders from competing companies and other organizations to speak to your managers.

- **REWARD THE EMPLOYEES WHO BRING IN THE BEST IDEAS.** To reinforce your commitment to learning and adopting a Best Practices mentality, consider offering added incentives to those employees who bring in ideas that add to revenues and/or productivity.

- **CELEBRATE NEW IDEAS.** Welch said that GE celebrated new ideas. Honor the best ideas by putting them online or in the company newsletter. This will underscore the company's commitment to an idea-oriented culture.

THE FOUR CHARACTERISTICS
OF A LEARNING ORGANIZATION

Although the road to a learning culture is unique to each organization, all learning cultures share certain characteristics. Here are four such traits:

1. **INFORMATION IS SHARED AND ACCESSIBLE.** In a learning culture, data and information are not kept secret or hoarded by management. Instead, they are readily accessible, so that managers and employees share a common frame of reference.

2. **LEARNING IS EMPHASIZED AND VALUED.** In a learning organization, training and learning are high priorities. At GE, Welch never stopped communicating this fundamental message, investing more than half a billion dollars per year in training and learning in the 1990s. By 2002, the year following Welch's retire-

ment, GE estimated that it was spending about *$1 billion* per year on training and training-related activities.

3. **MISTAKES OR FAILURES ARE NOT PUNISHED.** In a learning culture, it is okay to fail while trying new things. The key is to learn from those mistakes, so that the organization does not repeat them. This is an important characteristic of a learning organization. Nothing stifles innovation faster than punishing those who come up with ideas that do not work out.

4. **PEOPLE ARE EXPECTED TO LEARN CONSTANTLY.** Learning must be a part of the culture. In other words, it must be a reflex or a habit, not something that is practiced sporadically. It is incumbent upon managers to communicate this to employees, and to lead by example.

CREATING A LEARNING INFRASTRUCTURE

Welch did not start as GE's chairman with the notion of creating the world's largest learning organization, nor did that accomplishment come easily or quickly. It took many years, lots of sweat and blood, and a series of courageous decisions in the intervening years. He *did*, however, send the right message almost from the very start: Training would be a top priority at a Welch-headed General Electric.

When Welch became chairman in 1981, he inherited a company that he felt was in dire need of a dramatic overhaul. Vowing to launch a revolution, he sold off businesses, laid off more than 100,000 workers, removed layers of management, and subjected GE's remaining businesses to new performance standards (be number one or number two in your market, or you will be fixed, closed, or sold). Here's how he summarized those early years, looking back from the vantage point of 2001:

Like most American companies, we had built a military industrial complex . . . we had these layers and layers and layers of bureaucracy on top of people. We had people writing reports to each other. Instead of growing, we were managing growth. I just thought that we had to get the people off the people.

Welch's leadership ideal was formed during his first days at GE, in the early 1960s, when he worked in a small lab in the plastics business. There was no bureaucracy, business was fast and exciting, and there were no management layers to clog up decision making. He believed that re-creating that small-company ideal (which he later compared to a corner grocery store) was the key to enhancing productivity and creating a learning culture in a vast bureaucracy like GE. At the corner grocery, the owner knows the customers, knows what they want, and even knows why they buy what they buy. Welch thought his mammoth corporation could, and should, move in that direction.

Many of his most important initiatives were aimed at removing roadblocks to productivity ("get the people off the people") in an effort to reach his ultimate goal: a company devoid of bureaucracy and boundaries, in which ideas and intellect would rule. But it would take years to create that model. First, he had to attend to more immediate matters.

One of those more urgent matters was getting expenses under control. Although Welch's early moves involved massive restructuring and cost cutting, he invested more than $45 million to upgrade Crotonville, GE's famed management development center on the Hudson. While many insiders second-guessed this priority, Welch was undeterred. He knew that his transformation of GE would require a home base. From that point on, Crotonville served as the focal point of his self-proclaimed revolution.

It was at Crotonville, for example, that GE trained thousands of managers in the latest company idea or initiative (such as Six Sigma, digitization, and so on). Investing in Crotonville was an important first move, but developing an authentic learning culture within such a huge corporation would require many more crucial and difficult steps.

A ROAD MAP FOR CREATING A LEARNING ORGANIZATION

Nearly every move that Welch made in his far-reaching effort to reinvent GE had both intended and unintended consequences. For instance, his restructuring/downsizing phase strengthened the organization's financials, but had a negative impact on morale. This had two important implications for the learning-organization initiatives. First, the organization had to keep a watchful eye out for unintended consequences. And second, the organization had to be willing to accept risk and learn from its mistakes—including mistakes in the way it learned and the way it acted on the knowledge that it acquired. For most large companies, in other words, there is simply no fast track to embedding a learning culture into the fabric of the organization. In the case of GE, Welch had to perform a myriad of different tasks and initiatives, learning as he went, before he could call his creation a genuine learning culture.

Welch's long path to building a high-octane, performance-based learning culture provides clues for others who are attempting to create a similar culture within their own organization. However, as noted earlier, no two enterprises are alike. While these steps made sense for GE, many other factors—such as existing norms and culture, company history, management beliefs, and so on—could make these steps less applicable in other situations.

The following steps are presented in summary form. They represent what Welch did in his "business laboratory" (a favorite Welch term) at GE over a 20-year period, from 1981 to 2001. They are less a comprehensive blueprint than a general framework.

1. MAKE SURE THE COMPANY IS FINANCIALLY SOUND BEFORE EMBARKING ON SOMETHING AS SWEEPING AS DEVELOPING A LEARNING CULTURE. As discussed earlier, Welch's first priority was to put the company on a sound financial footing. He knew he could not start by creating a learning culture. Lagging businesses and a bloated bureaucracy were weighing down the company and preventing it from moving forward. While the company was widely perceived as doing well, he felt that there were too many layers, too many managers, and so on. This is why he implemented massive cost cutting and restructuring during his self-proclaimed "hardware phase."

Most companies today are far leaner than the GE of 1981, with its 25,000 managers and dozens of layers of management. But the principle remains the same: Unless a company is on firm financial footing (i.e., a strong balance sheet, income statement, etc.), establishing a learning culture may be difficult, or even counterproductive. It's important to get one's house in order first.

2. **SET A DEFINITIVE STRATEGIC DIRECTION, AND MAKE SURE THAT THE VISION IS ARTICULATED THROUGHOUT THE ORGANIZATION.** In the mid-1980s, Welch made sure that the company had a sound vision and a sound growth strategy. For example, he decided that all of GE's businesses should fit into his "three circles" vision (core, technology, or service), and he made acquisition and divestment decisions based on this strategy.

In 1986, Welch bought RCA for $6 billion, thereby acquiring NBC for the company and making GE one of the nation's top service companies. This was a pivotal move in transforming GE from an aging industrial manufacturer into an agile service provider with significant growth potential. (GE Capital, the company's financial services arm, delivered about half of the profits of the entire company in 2002.)

One important point: Welch made all of his restructuring moves *in full view*. Many insiders were not happy about his drastic changes. But they understood his vision and, despite their discomfort with many of his innovations, were able to make sense of the larger picture that was coming together.

Welch made other strategic decisions as well. One of the most important was his "number one, number two" strategy, which raised the bar for all of GE's businesses. He also let it be known that he was aiming for nothing less than the world's most competitive organization—a declaration that said a great deal about Welch's seriousness and determination.

3. **MAKE SURE THAT THERE IS A STATED SET OF VALUES TO GUIDE THE COMPANY.** This was a key management tool that Welch used to make sure that all managers and employees were on the same page in terms of company priorities and goals. Developing a learning culture is difficult without a common set of values and principles to guide the company. Also make sure that there is a mechanism to communicate these values, and a culture in place that reinforces them.

The value set served as a sort of "constitution" at GE, helping to guide the company through the many changes that it experienced under Welch. It was amended from time to time to reflect the latest GE priority or companywide initiative. In 1985, for example, GE's values included statements like "change is continual" and "paradox is a way of life." In 2002, by contrast, GE's stated values included having "passion for customers" (which was number one), "every person, every idea counts," and "playing offense." Welch viewed these values as such a key part of his cultural vision that he said that managers who could not live up to them should be fired, even if they made their financial goals.

4. **ESTABLISH AN ENVIRONMENT OF TRUST AND OPEN-NESS.** In his self-proclaimed "software phase," Welch strove to establish an atmosphere of trust—something that was sorely lacking in the wake of all the bloodletting associated with the hardware phase. At that point, many GE-ers feared for their futures and had little trust in management. At the same time, Welch concluded that managers were not listening to workers in any meaningful way. He knew that without a meaningful dialogue between managers and workers, things had little chance to get much better.

The situation was, in other words, a powder keg. With so many fewer workers now on the payroll, Welch knew that he needed more from the "survivors" than ever before. As a result of management's actions (including Welch's own), however, these workers lacked confidence and felt that their ideas didn't matter. Welch knew that confidence was key, which is why he set out to completely overhaul the company's hidebound, antiquated culture. This is when Welch's signature concept—Work-Out, described next—was born.

5. **CREATE A "BOUNDARYLESS ORGANIZATION."** By 1989, having concluded that managers were not talking with employees, Welch knew he needed a program or initiative that would put an end to this state of affairs. Those who did the work, Welch argued, had some striking ideas on how to make things better. This was the impetus for Welch's cultural initiative, Work-Out, which turned hierarchy on its head by

compelling managers to listen to employees and to
their ideas about how to improve things. In a Work-
Out session, typically lasting 3 days, workers made
suggestions to the bosses on how to improve
processes and other important work flow issues, and
managers had to say "yes," "no," or "I'll get back to
you within this specific period of time." The result?
At the typical session, managers said "yes," on the
spot, *80 percent of the time.*

Work-Out was instrumental in moving the organization closer to Welch's organizational ideal,
which he dubbed "boundaryless" (he admitted that
it was a strange word). Boundaryless enterprises
eliminate the walls that traditionally separate managers from employees, marketing from manufacturing, and employees from customers. "Every wall is
a bad one," proclaimed Welch, who set his sights on
creating an organization characterized by its trust,
openness and candor. Work-Out was the key to
jump-starting this movement, which played out
during the late 1980s and early to mid-1990s. During this period, the vast majority of GE employees
and managers attended multiple Work-Out sessions.

6. MAKE SPEED, FLEXIBILITY, AND INNOVATION A REFLEX.
Three characteristics of the boundaryless organization are speed, flexibility, and innovation. If the
members of your management team don't use these
words to describe your company, then it is likely that
you have some distance to go on the path to bound-
arylessness.

Speed: In an organization with speed, the workers closest to the work get things done quickly. Customer needs are addressed on the spot, and information and ideas flow easily between units—whether they are across the hall or around the globe.

Flexibility: In a boundaryless organization, managers routinely exhibit flexibility in order to get the job done. For example, after Welch launched his Six Sigma initiative in 1986, hundreds of managers switched jobs to become full-time quality professionals. This would not have been possible in an inflexible organization.

Innovation: In an enterprise that lives innovation, new ideas are valued and acted on quickly. Managers and employees at all levels are expected to be innovative. New ideas for products or processes do not require multiple levels of approval.

The key is to have workers feel empowered to move quickly and to make important decisions without having to obtain multiple approvals. It is also crucial that workers not fear retribution for making a wrong call. Smaller organizations and start-ups act quickly, and for years, Welch said that he wanted to instill a small-company spirit into the big body of GE. Small firms know the penalty for hesitating in the marketplace, exclaimed Welch; GE should behave in exactly the same way.

7. MAKE SURE THAT EVERYONE IN YOUR ORGANIZATION IS ENCOURAGED TO SEEK OUT THE BEST IDEAS FROM ANY-WHERE. As Welch has said many times, it is a badge of honor to get good ideas from someone else. For

example, he is the first to admit that Six Sigma, the statistically based quality program that he made wildly popular, was pioneered not by him or by GE, but by the electronics manufacturer Motorola. The key is to make sure that people in your organization search out new ideas from everywhere, especially from competitors. In a learning organization, it is the responsibility of every employee to learn and to constantly monitor the environment for new ideas.

8. **IMPLEMENT A BEST PRACTICES PROGRAM—IMPORTING THE BEST IDEAS SHOULD BE A PROCESS, NOT SIMPLY A MIND-SET.** Best Practices is the most efficient way to do something and a vital piece of a learning organization. Under Welch's guidance, GE began to systematically roam the world, learning "better ways of doing things from the world's best companies." In late 1989, Welch launched a comprehensive Best Practices movement that featured 3-day workshops.

To make sure that GE learned from the right companies, he assigned the task of finding world-class companies to emulate to one of his top business-development managers. (Ford and Hewlett-Packard were among the first companies studied.) Welch described GE as "a high spirited, endlessly curious enterprise," one that was dedicated to finding the best people and "cultivating in them an insatiable appetite to learn, to stretch, and to find that better idea, that better way, every day."

9. **REWARD BEHAVIORS AND ACTIONS THAT PROMOTE A LEARNING CULTURE.** Welch decided that it was vital

for the company's compensation and reward systems to be in alignment with the company's goals. Accordingly, he urged his business leaders to align rewards with outcomes—and he led by example. When he became CEO, stock options were restricted to a few hundred top executives of the company. By the time he left, more than 30,000 GE managers were participating in GE's lucrative stock option program.

10. **ESTABLISH PROCESSES AND AN INFRASTRUCTURE FOR CONVERTING LEARNING INTO RESULTS.** In order to make sure that learning and intellect are shared throughout the organization, management needs to hold regularly scheduled meetings, reviews, training sessions, courses, and so on. This was one of the chief purposes of Crotonville, which provides training to more than 7000 GE managers annually. Again, Welch led by example: Not only was he a frequent visitor to GE's learning institute, but he also taught there. (Welch holds a Ph.D. in chemical engineering.)

Welch called GE's learning infrastructure its "operating system," and he described the operating system as "GE's learning culture in action." The operating system refers to a system of intense learning sessions in which the key unit leaders and "initiative champions" from both inside and outside GE get together to share ideas and discuss the company's key initiatives.

11. **USE COMPANYWIDE INITIATIVES TO SPREAD THE GOSPEL.** During his tenure, Welch launched five

sweeping companywide initiatives that forever changed what Welch referred to as the DNA of the corporation: globalization, Work-Out (the company's only cultural initiative), services, Six Sigma (a quality program), and digitization (e-business). In order to launch these comprehensive programs, Welch created a far-reaching apparatus to help spread the message about—and train managers in—the latest initiative.

These initiatives helped to make GE a cohesive organization, rather than simply a collection of disparate companies. Welch called GE's high-involvement learning culture its "social architecture," and was proud of the fact that he was able to "involve everyone in the game." Welch said that involving everyone was one of the real keys to productivity, and that a company could get better as it got bigger simply because more people meant more ideas. This was Welch's thinking in his final year as CEO.

Despite the diversity of GE's businesses (which included everything from credit cards to gas turbines to NBC), Welch was able to get more than 300,000 employees marching to the same tune at the same time. GE's growth initiatives are credited with making the company more productive and more profitable. Under Welch, operating margins almost doubled, inventory turns increased dramatically, and GE achieved double-digit growth for two consecutive decades.

Welch's growth initiatives are given credit for being the keys to GE's transformation. Welch implemented these programs by driving them through the GE operating system. These initiatives, when combined with other Welch concepts and strategies, helped him to create more shareholder wealth than virtually any other CEO in history. When he took over, GE's total market capitalization was $13 billion. In the spring of 2000, GE became the most valuable company in the world, worth an astounding $596 billion (before sliding substantially in the market downturn of 2001 and 2002). There is little doubt that Welch's learning culture played a prominent role in GE's transformation from aging manufacturing bureaucracy to one of the world's largest, most valuable global multinationals.

POTENTIAL ROADBLOCKS TO SUSTAINING A LEARNING CULTURE

Creating a learning culture almost always involves a massive effort, and this is especially true if it's necessary to *re-create* the culture of an existing organization. If you decide to embark on the path of developing a learning culture, pay close attention to these potential stumbling blocks:

- A BLOATED BUREAUCRACY. Nothing can slow an organization down faster than bureaucracy. Welch hated bureaucracy from the start, urging all managers to "fight it, kick it." Disdaining bureaucracy was one of the key GE values for years, and many of GE's key tactics and programs were aimed at eliminating unnecessary layers of management, needless approvals, and anything else that slowed the company down. Welch worked for years to replace GE's pervasive bureaucracy with trust, excitement, and informality.

- **AN ENTRENCHED CULTURE, MIRED IN THE PAST.** How do most large companies get things done? The answer is: *Our way.* Transforming an organization almost always includes transforming the culture, which means changing the old mind-set. This is one of the most difficult aspects of leading any large-scale change in an organization. Welch was able to accomplish this through Work-Out, the GE values, eliminating non-performers (the bottom 10 percent), and constantly communicating the message.

- **GETTING THE SEQUENCE WRONG.** It would make little sense to attempt any large-scale change in a company that is about to be restructured or significantly downsized. An organization needs to be relatively stable before a learning infrastructure can be established. Otherwise, employees and managers alike will have a difficult time focusing on the task at hand, because they will be (correctly) absorbed with fixing the problems that are plaguing the corporation.

- **TRYING TO DO TOO MUCH, TOO SOON.** The road to a learning organization involves many steps that are likely to require years, not months, to implement. In today's turbulent, short-term-oriented business environment, many business leaders may not have the time to do what Welch did. In today's corporate world, missing a quarterly profit goal by even a modest amount can send the company's stock plummeting by 20, 30, or even 40 percent. (It's an expectations game, as much as anything else.) Given that unforgiving reality, an impatient CEO may decide to move too quickly, skip steps, or assume that creating a few training courses is tantamount to creating a learning culture. While there is nothing inherently wrong with training—in fact, it is a vital part of the learning infrastructure—it is only a small part of the larger change effort.

- **LETTING DOWN YOUR GUARD.** Managers who lead learning organizations cannot afford to get complacent or let down their guard. Learning must remain a top priority, and the message must be delivered consistently. Managers must send the message that learning is the key to the future, and that message must be backed up by the company's promotion and compensation systems.

What Would Jack Welch Do?

Depending upon your perspective, the case that started this chapter is either the simplest of the cases in this book or the biggest curve ball of the bunch. Unlike the other six scenarios, this one is really not fictitious, as it almost exactly describes the situation that confronted Jack Welch when he took the reins at GE in 1981.

The company's growth goal prior to Welch was to grow at a faster rate than the economy, making it a slightly-better-than-GNP company. There were more than 25,000 managers, and strategic planners often told the leaders how their businesses should be run. Managers weren't talking to employees, which helps to explain why they knew little about the morale of the workers. Many businesses at GE were limping along, at best. As a result of these and other problems, GE had lost half of its stock market value (when adjusted for inflation) in the decade prior to Welch's appointment.

What would Jack Welch do? In this particular case, we *know* what he did. He sold off losing businesses, kept and acquired market-leading businesses, fired the strategic planners, and worked every day to reduce bureaucracy. (Welch once compared bureaucracy to Dracula, saying that even after you've conquered it, it rises from the dead.) He spent years establishing an organization that thrived on trust and candor, and valued ideas over rank. He used growth initiatives to make the company more competitive, simultaneously ensuring that all of GE's diverse businesses operated from the same playbook. He took the concept of leadership to a new level, and never stopped trying to improve things.

Welch raised the bar on multiple fronts. For example, in his view, double-digit growth was the only acceptable growth measurement. And he worked feverishly to knock down as many boundaries as he could, and to install in their place a *learning infrastructure* that would help the company gather and implement strong new ideas.

ASSESS YOUR CEO QUOTIENT

1. How much bureaucracy is there in your organization? Are too many required approvals and permission-seeking activities slowing decision-making?

2. How well do your managers know their employees? Is there a healthy and honest dialogue, or are managers simply giving directives and expecting workers to carry them out?

3. Are training and learning high priorities in your organization?

4. Are the values of the company clearly stated? Do most workers know what these values are and live by them?

5. Are employees and managers alike encouraged to seek out the best ideas from everywhere?

6. Is there a system or infrastructure in place that allows senior managers to drive an idea or initiative through every part of the company (i.e., through every business, layer, geographic location, etc.)?

MORE LESSONS FROM THE CEO

1. **MAKE SURE THAT THE ENTIRE ORGANIZATION KNOWS OF YOUR COMMITMENT TO LEARNING.** Meet with your key managers, and make sure they get the message. Also make sure that the message gets to the rest of the company (via speeches, emails, memos, etc.). Never miss an opportunity to get the word out: From this point forward, learning will be the rule, not the exception.

2. **BACK UP YOUR WORDS WITH ACTION.** As discussed throughout the chapter, a proper learning infrastructure is a key prerequisite of a learning culture. In order to build the infrastructure, you'll need to make sure that the business is healthy, there is a minimum of bureaucracy, you have a top-tier team of managers and employees throughout the organization, and so on.

3. **REMOVE BARRIERS TO PRODUCTIVITY.** Anything that comes between employees and getting the job done in an open organization should be removed. This means ridding the organization of red tape and bureaucracy at every level—a large task in itself, involving everything from restructuring to Work-Out-type meetings to establishing trust by sharing information.

4. **IF YOUR COMPANY DOES NOT HAVE AN ARTICULATED SET OF COMPANY VALUES, ESTABLISH A SMALL TASK FORCE TO CREATE ONE.** Values can be key in guiding a company, but only if they are the right ones. Make sure that you get the right people working on this, under your leadership, and that the values they define are the principles that best represent the spirit of the company.

5. **START A "BEST PRACTICES" MOVEMENT.** Best Practices is one of the hallmarks of a learning culture. Assign at least one key senior manager the job of finding the best companies to study and emulate. Let it be

known that Best Practices will be an important part of the company culture.

6. **CONSIDER IMPLEMENTING COMPANYWIDE INITIATIVES.** While not every company is able to launch programs like Six Sigma with the success enjoyed by GE, Welch proved that if executed properly, such initiatives can reduce costs, enhance productivity, and add value to an organization. The key is making sure that the initiatives you introduce are the right ones for *your* organization—and, of course, that they are executed with skill and precision.

CHAPTER 4

Focus on Solutions

IBM is a solutions company. We start with a customer's business problem, and work back to the right combination of technologies and expertise.

—Lou Gerstner, former CEO, IBM

So there was IBM, the company that had led the prior phase of computing and had invented many of the industry's most important technologies, crawling out of bed every morning to find its relevance marginalized by the darlings of desktop computing.

—LOU GERSTNER, March 2002

What Would Lou Gerstner Do?

In the seat of the CEO: You are the senior partner of a
three-person law firm in a large town located within 30
miles of Chicago. You started the business more than 20
years ago, after spending 10 years working your way up the
ladder of one of Chicago's hottest law firms. Rather than go
the partner route, you decided to hang out your own
shingle back in your hometown.

At first, the bulk of your business involved closings and
other real estate transactions. Because the town had been
mostly farmland for a century, your practice thrived, since
there were many new homes popping up and there was
strong demand for a sharp attorney who knew the real
estate market. The growth of the residential population
enticed several new small businesses to set up shop in the
area, so you soon brought two new attorneys into the
practice: one who could help with the backlog of residential
and commercial real estate closings, and another who
specialized in legal services for small businesses. Over the
next decade, your firm became one of the best known and
most successful in "town," which now had more than
100,000 citizens.

During the last 2 years, however, business has slowed
dramatically. This is puzzling. After all, the town has never
been stronger economically, as three *Fortune 500* companies
have moved major operations into the town, providing
thousands of new jobs. The expanding presence of those
companies has attracted younger people, both single and
married, into the community, and you've been assuming
that the influx of new homeowners would send your real
estate business soaring. That's not happening. These

s aren't approaching your firm for legal services,
real estate–related or otherwise.

p get to the bottom of this mystery, you meet with
your two fellow attorneys to discuss the situation. None of
you can figure out what's going wrong. After all, your firm
has been on top for years, and it has undeniably established
the reputation of being the best around in real estate law.
But business continues to fall off—so dramatically, in fact,
that there is not enough work for all of you.

Reluctantly, you let one of the other attorneys go. You
know that unless things improve soon, you will be forced to
let the other one go as well.

What has happened? What accounts for the drop-off in
business? What do you do?

What would Lou Gerstner do?

Thomas Watson, the founding genius of one of the
largest corporate entities ever assembled, once told his
colleagues to "aim high, and think in big figures."

When he referred to "big figures," Watson surely was
not thinking of big *losses*. But that was exactly what corporate colossus IBM was facing in 1993. And it wasn't just a
run-of-the-mill big loss, but the largest annual loss in corporate history to date—an eye-popping $8.1 billion.

The once-dominant computer company not only was
deep in the red, but was sinking under the weight of its
own ineptitude. The industry's long-time leader had failed
to grasp the changes transforming the computer industry,
and was thoroughly demoralized. Andy Grove of Intel said,
"It's hard to describe how beaten down that company

was." The IBM board, in desperate need of a new leader, put together a short list that included corporate heavyweights such as Jack Welch, Bill Gates, and Ross Perot. Ultimately, however, they zeroed in on Louis V. Gerstner, CEO of RJR Nabisco.

When the announcement came that IBM's board had named a former snack-food king to succeed John Akers (IBM's previous CEO, whom many had blamed for the company's troubles), the response was a mix of disbelief and consternation. Wall Street sneered, company insiders grumbled, and just about everyone was convinced that the board had made a huge mistake. (Even Gerstner later admitted that he, too, was afraid that the board had made a mistake.) Critics derided Gerstner for his lack of experience running a technology company, much less the world's most important computer manufacturer.

The Gerstner-bashing, spearheaded by the media, went on for weeks. The press questioned Gerstner's fitness for the position. In Q&A sessions, media representatives peppered him with questions intended to test his readiness for the top post at IBM—and perhaps even to trip him up. But Gerstner (publicly, at least) demonstrated guts and patience. For example, when asked for his vision of the future IBM, he responded:

The last thing IBM needs now is a vision.

The company was hemorrhaging, and Gerstner knew that he had to apply tourniquets before planning the patient's future. He had to pull off the greatest turnaround in corporate history—but first, he had to make sure that the company would not be torn into pieces.

ONE IBM IS BETTER THAN EIGHT

In December of 1992, IBM's then CEO John Akers developed a plan to break up his company into several smaller units. The plan—to some extent motivated by the Justice Department–inspired break-up of the Bell system into the "Baby Bells"—had many advocates, especially within the company. With IBM in such dire straits, many insiders believed that several independent units (dubbed the "Baby Blues") competing *against* one another would have a better chance at surviving. But Gerstner's first major decision, upon taking up the reins, went in the opposite direction. He decided *not* to break up the company, arguing that implementing the plan would "splinter [IBM] into a collection of piece-part providers":

> *There wasn't going to be an IBM; there was going to be six or eight IBMs—effectively no IBM. So we made the very early decision— the most important decision I'll ever make in my business career— to reverse that direction and keep IBM whole.*

Gerstner made this decision after spending his first months on the job racking up tens of thousands of air miles as he met with customers and managers all over the world. At the end of this odyssey, he was convinced that IBM's hoped-for resurrection would depend on the company's ability to provide a full range of computer products and solutions, rather than simply providing hardware or software. If IBM could do that, customers would look to it to solve *all* of their computer problems, not just provide piecemeal equipment or stopgap IT measures.

What customers needed, Gerstner said, was "somebody who could sit in the middle of a lot of very-difficult-to-integrate technology and pull it all together . . . an integrator who could translate all the technologies into business value."

The alternative [to breaking up the company] was to keep IBM together and to make the breadth of our products, services, and skills our most potent competitive advantage.

In reaching this momentous decision, Gerstner unwittingly played out one of IBM founder Thomas Watson's favorite maxims: "Don't talk machines, talk the prospect's business." And while his own investigations proved critical, the new CEO now needed every part of IBM in order to talk to prospects and find new ways to define and solve their business problems.

The lessons from Gerstner's first months on the job provide valuable insights for other managers grappling with difficult challenges:

- USE EVERY WEAPON IN YOUR ARSENAL. Gerstner knew that he needed all of IBM in order to transform the company, which explains why he kept the company whole. The same lesson pertains even at moderate-sized companies. Make sure that you use every part of the company when you are rethinking corporate strategy or making other far-reaching changes. In these turbulent times, you cannot afford to leave any division, unit, or individual on the sidelines.

- **LET THE CUSTOMER IDENTIFY YOUR ACHILLES HEEL.** Gerstner knew that the company was in dire straits. In his conversations with customers around the world, he acknowledged that painful fact and asked the customers where the company had gone wrong. That is a key lesson. Your managers and employees may know a great deal about the company, but your customers will provide a fresh perspective.

- **GET YOUR FINANCIAL HOUSE IN ORDER AND FINALIZE YOUR VISION BEFORE YOU IMPLEMENT ANY SWEEPING NEW PLAN.** When Gerstner declared, "The last thing IBM needs now is a vision," he was focusing on the billions of dollars the company was losing annually. He knew that he had to lead the company out of the "abyss" first. Only after implementing severe cost-cutting measures did he turn his attention to transforming the company culture and developing the vision of IBM as a global solutions company.

PUT A CUSTOMER IN THE CEO'S OFFICE

But Gerstner knew he had to go far beyond simply keeping the company together. He knew that a dramatic shift in mind-set and culture would be a key prerequisite for any sustained turnaround. Through his personal observations, he had determined that the company's insularity and arrogance had helped to fuel its downfall—that the company's long run of success was part of the reason for its failings. Here's how he put it (in an interview with the author) in 2002:

IBM had enjoyed such a long run . . . that people began to look around for their next real challenge, and started finding it inside the company, rather than in the marketplace. The entire focus shifted from customers to a series of intramural competitions.

In other words, IBM had turned inward. Arrogantly, it assumed that it needed no help in figuring out what to do next. It didn't need to study competitors, survey the marketplace, or respond to the massive changes that were transforming the industry. It could, and did, focus on internal squabbles and turf wars, assuming that the outside world would always turn to Big Blue for help.

It was a bad bet, and now the company was on the rocks. This in itself was a problem so severe that it threatened the company's future. Gerstner believes that every time a company gets into real trouble, "virtually all the management focus turns to 'the problem.' It freezes organizations." Big changes were needed, and fast.

Gerstner boldly decided that he would transform the culture "around three key attributes: marketplace obsession, speed, and teamwork." Gerstner knew that one of his top priorities was to get the company to shift its attention to the customer:

In the spring of 1993, a big part of what I had to do was get the company refocused on the marketplace as the only valid measure of success. I started telling virtually every audience . . . that there was a customer running IBM, and that we were going to rebuild the company from the customer back.

Gerstner felt that he could not emphasize this point often enough or loudly enough. Transforming the company from an "inwardly focused organization" to one that was focused on the marketplace and customer solutions was "absolutely critical to everything else we had to do to transform IBM." His key message throughout the first 6 months of his tenure was that IBM was going to make sure that it was the customers that drove the company, not the other way around.

One of the key measures that Gerstner took in helping to change the focus from "inside-out" to "outside-in" was to turn to an *outsider* for help. According to one former IBM senior executive, in 1993 Gerstner brought in Jack Welch on the night he launched his transformation/reengineering effort at IBM's education center in Palisades.

After Welch shared his GE experience with Big Blue's top-tier managers, Gerstner challenged his executives to meet some "heroic" objectives of their own, including taking $1.5 billion out of the company's run rate that same year (and this was a midyear meeting). One executive who attended that now-infamous meeting described Gerstner's gut-wrenching request as "shock treatment," and also said that it was Gerstner's way of encouraging "out-of-the-box thinking" and instilling a new sense of urgency. The IBM executives got the message, and later implemented other "Welch-like" measures, such as eliminating the bottom 10 percent of the workforce.

In retrospect, Gerstner says that the decision to keep IBM intact and the effort to reestablish the primacy of the customer were not separate initiatives. They were, as he sees it, two sides of the same coin, and together they set the stage for IBM's dramatic comeback.

Again in retrospect, Gerstner calls the task of bringing about cultural change "mind-bendingly hard" and "frustrating." Changing an entrenched large-company culture and transforming the prevailing mind-set from *selling products* to *providing solutions* was a process that took years, and its progress was often measured in inches. When asked what advice he would give other managers attempting to change the culture of an organization, he replied with the following:

> *Be patient. By that, I don't mean be complacent. . . . It takes time. And the progress, in my experience, is always going to come slower than you want. By the way, that assumes that you know what you want when you start, which I'd assert is one reason so few attempts at broad-based cultural change ever really pay off: lack of clarity about what success is going to look like.*

Once again, Gerstner's words and actions provide a rough blueprint for other companies faced with the challenge of transforming their culture:

- **GET THE COMPANY TO LOOK OUTSIDE OF THE COMPANY FOR ANSWERS.** Once the leaders of an organization realize that the ship is on the rocks, there is a real risk that they will freeze the learning process. Emphasize the importance of focusing on customers and the marketplace, and lead by example, spending time learning from competitors and meeting with key customers.

- **TO TRANSFORM THE COMPANY MIND-SET, CONSIDER GER-STNER'S THREE KEYS: MARKETPLACE OBSESSION, SPEED, AND TEAMWORK.** These were the principles that Gerstner employed in creating a new IBM. These timeless ideas are as relevant in a small shop as they are in a large multinational.

- **UNDERSTAND THAT GENUINE CULTURAL CHANGE CAN TAKE YEARS.** Remember that Gerstner felt the enormous challenge of changing the company's culture was one of its greatest hurdles. That's particularly true in a huge company like IBM, but it also applies to smaller firms. Exercise patience when attempting meaningful change. (This is a recurring theme with virtually every one of the companies featured in this book.)

GAINING THE SOLUTIONS EDGE

Early in his tenure, the new IBM chief set his sights on expenses. Desperate to get costs under control, Gerstner eliminated 60,000 jobs in his first year as CEO, using the blunt instruments of layoffs and early retirements to transform IBM's unyielding white-shirt culture. Jumping to the punch line, the effort (and related efforts) was a spectacular success: Within 5 years (that is, by 1998), Gerstner had turned $16 billion of *losses* into a $5 billion *gain*. This was the most sweeping corporate turnaround of all time.

Gerstner did not achieve this spectacular success simply by selling more computers. He did it by transforming an old-economy hardware company into a reinvigorated organization—one that stressed solutions over hardware:

We've helped thousands of customers develop a network strategy that's right for them. This is what we mean when we say IBM is a solutions company. We start with a customer's business problem, and work back to the right combination of technologies and expertise.

One of the keys to the entire effort, said Gerstner, was what he called "technical integration"—that is, an "integration of hardware and software, integration of services and products, integration of client and server."

That's the big-picture view of Gerstner's successful effort to change the company to its core. But we need to look more closely at how he achieved this success. We need to dissect the specifics of the turnaround in order to see CEO Gerstner at work—his thinking processes, his tactics, and his strategies.

WHEN HARDWARE STALLS, TURN TO SERVICE

Gerstner knew that IBM's hardware business, which had carried the company for so long, was shrinking at an alarming rate. Within a 3-year span during the early 1990s, hardware sales dropped 50 percent, erasing more than $14 billion in hardware profits. Meanwhile, margins were thinning to an alarming degree. Although the company sold $12 billion worth of personal computers in 1993, those sales ended up putting the company far deeper in the red.

Following in the footsteps of GE's Jack Welch, IBM's new CEO set his sights on boosting the company's service businesses. Welch had proved that services could be the key to jump-starting a stagnant manufacturing business, and IBM—with an enormous base of still-loyal customers— was in an ideal position to take the same path. And although the IBM service businesses were started well before

Gerstner arrived, it was he who recognized, and acted upon, the tremendous growth potential of service:

Services is the fastest-growing part of the information technology industry, and our services business is growing 20 percent a year—and 50 percent faster than the overall industry. One of the things we like best about this opportunity is that it's big—twice as big as hardware, and there is no dominant competitor. At least not yet.

But the shift to being a services-oriented company meant an enormous change for IBM. Henceforth, the company would have to acknowledge the existence of its competitors—with whom it had traditionally had bad relations—and work with them to provide customers with better solutions. "The customer would not accept a services company if all it did was flog IBM products," explained Gerstner. But forging relationships with the companies that had toppled IBM off its accustomed pedestal was anathema to IBM traditionalists. In fact, recalls Gerstner, his decision to move into services "set off an incredible bomb in the company. Here was a part of IBM that was going to work closely with Oracle, Sun Microsystems, and, God forbid, Microsoft."

But Gerstner's bet on services was both smart and well timed. By the time he retired in March of 2002, services were delivering approximately half of the company's sales and profits. IBM's Global Services Business, the company's single largest business, helped IBM "look at technology through the eyes of the customer" and played a significant role in fulfilling Gerstner's goal of a market-obsessed IBM.

Gerstner's decision to develop IBM's service business holds several important business lessons worth noting here:

- **BE SURE TO MONITOR THE GROWTH OF YOUR CORE BUSINESS AND OTHER KEY BUSINESSES.** Gerstner could not help but know that hardware sales were shrinking dramatically. If and when *your* core business falters, it isn't likely to occur as quickly (IBM's hardware sales fell 50 percent in 3 years!). Since the signs are usually not that obvious, be sure to closely monitor your largest businesses, their closest competitors, and any other trends or signs that may affect these businesses now or sometime down the line.

- **DO NOT EXPECT MANAGERS AND EMPLOYEES TO READILY ACCEPT A SHIFT IN STRATEGY.** Remember that Gerstner said that the move to services "set off an incredible bomb" within IBM. Any substantial strategic change is likely to be resisted by those who have spent years doing things the old way. That is why it is so important to set the stage by working on changing the culture before implementing any major new strategic initiative. If that isn't possible, then work on culture and strategy simultaneously.

FROM BIG IRON TO E-BUSINESS JUGGERNAUT

The bold moves that Gerstner made early on proved that IBM's CEO was among the first leaders of long-established companies to grasp the mind-boggling potential of Internet technology. The IBM chief regards the Internet not as simply another new technology, but as the leading edge of a bona fide paradigm shift:

Every day it becomes more clear that the Net is taking its place alongside the other great transformational technologies that first challenged, and then fundamentally changed, the way things are done in the world.

Gerstner's $300 million Internet gambit, launched in 1995, gave IBM a decisive head start in the digital arena and helped it to transform itself from a mainframe company into a modern-day knowledge-based business. Gerstner knew that to complete the transformation, he would have to push the Internet into every nook and cranny of IBM, from its products to its practices and marketing.

He also knew that embracing the Internet created enormous challenges for most companies, and that the majority of organizations—including the majority of the organizations in IBM's client base—needed help in figuring it all out. This involved everything from selling existing products online to coming up with a cohesive Net strategy for the future. In short, these companies needed the new IBM to help them fully integrate the Internet into the way they did business every day:

The Internet is ultimately about innovation and integration. But you don't get the innovation unless you integrate Web technology into the processes by which you run your business.

By the late 1990s, evidence of IBM's transformation into a solutions provider was everywhere. By 2000, IBM was the top e-business solutions provider: It had an astounding 130,000 consultants who had completed 18,000 Internet service engagements in 3 years. Those assignments included everything from helping to create web site designs to devising entire Net strategies for its customers. This meant that IBM was doing *three times* more Net business than three of its larger competitors combined! Some $20 billion in revenues was derived from IBM's Internet initiative—proof positive that Gerstner's gambles on the Internet paid off.

INVEST IN R&D: THE SOLUTIONS PERSPECTIVE

Shortly after Gerstner arrived at IBM, he demonstrated his willingness to invest in the company's future, in the form of research and development, despite the company's mind-numbing losses. On the table was his predecessor's plan to dissolve IBM's research and development department. Again, Gerstner went in the opposite direction. He decided to keep the Watson Research Center (IBM's R&D lab) intact, and he instructed the researchers based there to spend more time on coming up with solutions to customers' problems.

Specifically, he pushed for R&D investments focused on the Internet. Gerstner recognized the incredible potential of the Internet as a driver of transactions early on, and he was so convinced of its potential that he was willing to reorganize the company around that idea:

> *If we really believe this, we're going to reprioritize all the budgets in the company. In a period of four weeks, we reallocated $300 million. We created the Internet division. It became the catalyst for change in the company.*

Gerstner calls this his second "bet the company" decision (the first was keeping the company intact). Early on, he shifted 25 percent of IBM's R&D into Net projects, and in 1999 he increased that percentage to 50 percent (and by then the R&D budget had grown to an impressive $5 billion).

Increased R&D expenditures were only the beginning. The IBM chief was fiercely determined to remake IBM into a provider of complete solutions and a leader in what he called "network computing." This was no fad or banner-waving exercise; instead, it was a company initiative designed to help the company remake itself:

> *The real leadership in the industry is moving away from the creation of the technology to the application of the technology.*

Here are some Gerstner-like activities that you could implement in your own organization:

- **INVEST IN THE FUTURE.** Regardless of the current market environment, companies cannot afford to be complacent. Make sure that your organization is betting on the future by making the right investments now.

- **WHEN MAKING "BET THE COMPANY" DECISIONS, MAKE SURE YOU'RE RIGHT.** Gerstner called his $300 million decision to create the Internet Division his second "bet the company" decision. While no one has a crystal ball, bet the company only when there is compelling evidence that your decision is the right one.

- **BE A TREND SPOTTER.** Gerstner recognized that the future of computing would depend on "moving away from the creation of the technology to the application of the technology." He was right, and his understanding of that fundamental shift in his industry played a role in the IBM turnaround.

Gerstner did so many things right, and—as noted—pulled off one of the great turnarounds in corporate history. Business historians may not rank him alongside Jack Welch or Bill Gates, but a compelling case can be made that he deserves a place in that pantheon. His rare ability to see a situation for what it was and then bring about meaningful change made him one of the most effective CEOs of his day.

What Would Lou Gerstner Do?

Returning to the scenario that opened the chapter, what explains the downfall of your law practice? The firm got into trouble because you and your partners failed to heed the seismic changes that were transforming your community.

Let's recap: For years, your law firm thrived on real estate closings and providing legal counsel for small businesses. In the first years of the practice, you responded to the needs of the community by adding attorneys who could address those specific needs.

In recent years, however, your firm hasn't kept up with the changes that were taking place in your town. The three large corporations that came to town altered the area's demographics, and, along with it, the type of legal services the community required. Those changes made your firm almost irrelevant, and because you looked to the other attorneys inside the firm rather than to the marketplace, you didn't understand what was happening.

For example, while some of the younger people who moved into the area bought homes, most of them rented condos or apartments, which diminished the town's need for attorneys who could handle closings. When these young singles started getting married and setting up households, they sought out firms that could handle wills, prenuptial agreements, and similar legal needs. Your firm was not prepared to offer this kind of specialized service.

Furthermore, the surge in the town's business activity was accompanied by an increase in workers' compensation claims, one more specialty your firm did not offer. Furthermore, many of your small clients disappeared, as large chains caused some independents to fail.

Ironically, your firm's success was a chief contributor to its downfall; it was at the top for so long that you stopped doing the things that got you there.

Your biggest sin was thinking that you had all the answers. You held internal meetings, rather than focus on the marketplace. Had you focused on the needs of the community, you and your partners would have recognized the shifting environment. Lou Gerstner would have made sure that the firm was well informed about the changing needs of the community. He would never have stopped thinking about ways to solve people's problems, even if that meant replacing attorneys who were unable to do so.

ASSESSING YOUR CEO QUOTIENT

1. Do you have a solutions mind-set or a product mind-set? If the answer is the latter, there may be some work in store for you and your team.

2. Do you have a customer in the CEO's office? If not, how much time do you and other top managers spend with customers?

3. Do you compete in an industry in which services and solutions can play a vital role? Is it likely that solutions will become more important in the months and years ahead?

4. If you answered yes to either part of question 3, on a scale of 1 to10, how does your company stack up in the solutions department?

5. Does your company currently derive fees from servicing existing products? How can that business be expanded?

6. Will knowledge-based products (consulting, e-solutions, etc.) replace existing products within your industry? If so, what can your company do to capitalize on this trend?

MORE LESSONS FROM THE CEO

1. **MAKE SURE THAT YOUR FIRM IS OBSESSED WITH YOUR CUSTOMERS.** Lead by example, and spend more time with customers. Remember that Gerstner and other top CEOs spend upwards of 50 percent of their time with customers. Many companies, even several of the best ones, suffer from NIH (not invented here). Make sure that your company adopts an outside-in perspective to counter NIH.

2. **TAKE A FEW MINUTES TO ASSESS YOUR INDUSTRY WITH A FRESH EYE.** Jot down four or five ways in which solutions and services will change your industry. Is there a possibility that your firm can either develop or expand its services component? Is there something that other managers (or past senior managers) may have missed?

3. **STUDY THE COMPETITIVE LANDSCAPE OF YOUR INDUSTRY BY SPENDING TIME ON YOUR COMPETITORS' WEB SITES, LOOKING AT THEIR NEW PRODUCTS, ETC.** How are your competitors making their businesses more solutions- and services-oriented? Incorporate the lessons you learn into your own company's playbook. Make a habit of this by allocating a portion of your time each week to studying the competition.

4. **IF APPLICABLE, WRITE DOWN FIVE TO SEVEN SOLUTIONS-ORIENTED PRODUCTS THAT YOUR COMPANY COULD CREATE WITHIN THE NEXT 3 YEARS.** This can include

servicing existing products. Make sure that these products are feasible given your company's product line and capabilities, and that they are consistent with the company's strategic direction.

5. **WORKING WITH THIS LIST, WRITE A MORE DETAILED BUSINESS PLAN DESCRIBING THE RESOURCES NEEDED TO CREATE THESE SOLUTIONS-ORIENTED PRODUCTS.** Be sure to include an analysis of the market (current and 3 years out), a detailed analysis of the competition, and revenue and profit potential. This need not be a 20-plus-page document; it can simply be a brief summary or a draft of a working plan. Be sure to include realistic timelines and revenue and profit assessments based on solid research.

6. **SHARE THIS PLAN WITH YOUR PEER MANAGERS AND BOSSES. ASK THEM FOR THEIR COMMENTS AND REACTIONS.** If your ideas are well received, work with other senior managers to implement the plans and expand your service/solutions business.

CHAPTER 5

Prepare the Organization for *Drastic* Change

Most companies don't die because they are wrong; most die because they don't commit themselves. They fritter away their momentum and their valuable resources while attempting to make a decision. The greater danger is in standing still.

—ANDY GROVE, cofounder and former CEO, Intel

I submit that all businesses, whether they are bricks origin or clicks origin, are today at a point of choice, such as a strategic inflection point and, depending on their embrace of the two elements. . . . They'll either write new competitive strategies or they'll be marginalized.

—ANDY GROVE

What Would Andy Grove Do?

In the seat of the CEO: You are the CEO of a midsized, publicly traded pharmaceutical maker based in the Midwest. While your firm produces more than 100 different drugs, it has become increasingly dependent on its runaway best-selling product, one of the top cholesterol-reducing drugs in the industry.

The drug, which last year enjoyed a 60 percent market share, is responsible for 80 percent of the company's profits. However, its share has fallen dramatically, as has investor confidence in your firm. The firm's stock price has plummeted approximately 50 percent from its recent highs, and with the stock slide, you have gone from hero to goat. Half a dozen Wall Street analysts have downgraded your stock, and the board is all over you, demanding to know what you intend to do about it.

What's behind the precipitous drop in market share? A supplement manufacturer (a company that was not even on your competitive radar screen) has produced a new supplement that has threatened your hold on the market. The new supplement contains antioxidants, garlic, ginger, and other curative herbs, and it appears to reduce cholesterol in middle-aged men and women without the side effects of drugs. To make matters worse, the retail price of the supplement is less than half the price of your fading star, and it requires no prescription.

Although you had heard talk about the therapeutic effects of herbs in reducing cholesterol, your key researchers advised you not to "concern yourself" with such alternatives. They agreed (as did your key managers) that garlic, supplements, and other such "mumbo jumbo" were nonsense, and would never catch on as viable competitors.

The sole dissenting voice in your firm was a junior researcher, but no one took him seriously enough to listen to him, despite his MIT degree.

The judgment of your management team appeared to be correct—until about 6 months ago, that is, when the supplement started to steal market share from your drug. Thanks to a two-page story in a national magazine (as well as Internet chat rooms that talked up the new "medical breakthrough"), the supplement took off. After the competing product reduced your market share by a third, you did some research of your own, and you discovered that, incredibly, there are more than 10,000 web sites devoted to cholesterol and its effect on health (including tips for reducing cholesterol, drug therapy, etc.).

Your new-product pipeline is relatively empty, and there certainly is nothing in it that can replace the lost revenue. Unless you are able to turn things around, you will report the worst financial quarter in the company's history. This will probably mean that the company will have to close plants and lay off thousands of workers. Where did you do wrong? Could this have been prevented? If so, how might it have been? And what do you do now?

What would Andy Grove do?

Few individuals have overcome more adversity than the Hungarian Jew Andras Grof. After nearly dying of scarlet fever and barely escaping the Nazis in World War II, he fled to the United States when the Red Army invaded his homeland. He taught himself English and worked his way through college in the United States, graduating from Berkeley.

In the late 1960s, he cofounded a small high-tech company named Intel. In 1997, *Time* magazine named him Person of the Year for his role in fueling the computer revolution. His personal mantra, "only the paranoid survive," helped him to survive and prosper throughout his career. Ironically, it just might have been Andras Grof's paranoid perspective that gave Andy Grove the foresight that he needed in order to help create an industry.

There is much to be learned from Grove's tumultuous journey toward building what would become the world's largest chipmaker. Along the way, his company confronted several crises of massive proportions. This reinforced and helps to explain his paranoid perspective. He once said, "Success breeds complacency. Complacency breeds failure." During his three-decade-plus career, Grove never had the luxury of complacency.

At least twice during his tenure, Intel faced challenges that could have crippled or destroyed the company. By clearing these hurdles successfully, Grove not only made his organization stronger and more resilient, but also contributed to the body of leadership knowledge, advancing a management construct that showed other managers how to deal with drastic change.

THE DUAL LEVERS OF SUCCESS: EXECUTION AND STRATEGY

It all started in 1968, when Grove teamed up with two other people who shared his vision for a new business. Andy Grove, Bob Noyce, and Gordon Moore thought they could own the world. They had discovered that they could store ever-increasing numbers of transistors on a single chip without noticeably increasing the costs. More transistors meant faster performance and more utility for computers (and, of course, for any other gizmo that used the chips). By creating chips that could store an ever-increasing amount of information, they could boost the computer's memory and functionality in an enormously cost-effective manner. Intel was born. And one of the most important things that it had going for it was Grove's common-sense wisdom:

I have a rule in my business: to see what can happen in the next ten years, look at what has happened in the last ten years.

Grove was not the only Intel manager with prescience. In 1975, Gordon Moore made a critical prediction of his own: He declared that the power of the computer chip would double every 18 months. That prediction, now called Moore's law, has proved remarkably accurate.

Grove built on Moore's law with a prophecy of his own: *The world will never stop finding new applications for these powerful chips.* With every new generation of computers, more powerful chips would be needed, and Intel would be the company that supplied them. Years later, Grove used a metaphor to describe how technology, manufacturing, and marketing provided the foundation for Intel's success:

The essence of a company like Intel is execution and strategy. Intel, looked at in another way, is a three-legged stool. One leg is technology—design and silicon technology—another leg is manufacturing, and the third leg is marketing. Whenever Intel did well it was because the three legs were equal. Whenever one of those legs was shorter than the others, we wobbled.

THE FIRST CRISIS: INTEL GETS BEATEN AT ITS OWN GAME

In the early 1980s, Intel's three-legged stool almost came crashing down. When the company first started, it had nearly a 100 percent share of the memory market. New competitors appeared in the 1970s, but it was not until the 1980s that the Japanese broke Intel's rock-solid hold on this market. They did so by producing chips that were not only superior in quality, but also lower in cost. Intel tried everything it could think of to battle the Japanese, but nothing worked. Grove later identified several factors that had contributed to Intel's misfortunes: The company had been late to market with several generations of products, and it hadn't invested in new factories early enough. Ultimately, though, the cause of the problem came down to the wrong strategy and poor execution:

You execute on the wrong strategy, you sink. You don't execute on the right strategy, you sink. . . . Actually, there's a perfect example of this: our performance in memory in the early '80s. Our execution and our strategy were faulty.

Intel had to do something to stop the bleeding. The company was losing money hand over fist, as demand for Intel's memory chips was in free fall. Grove felt the pressure: "The need for a different memory strategy, one that would stop the hemorrhage, was growing urgent."

Then one day in 1985, after Intel's problems had been raging for nearly a year, Grove found himself discussing the company's woes with Gordon Moore, then Intel's CEO. In that conversation, which was detailed in Grove's leadership memoir *Only the Paranoid Survive,* Grove asked Moore a question:

> *"If we got kicked out and the board brought in a new CEO, what do you think he would do?" Gordon answered without hesitation, "He would get us out of memories." I stared at him, numb, then said, "Why shouldn't you and I walk out the door, come back and do it ourselves?"*

This story has become an industry legend, and it is vintage Grove. He recognized that the Japanese competition was no ordinary threat. In fact, it was potent enough to put his company out of business. Even though Intel was built on a foundation of memory chips, the company really had no choice but to get out of this market. It simply could not continue on its current path. But Grove knew that abandoning the company's legacy would mean a long and difficult change process, almost certainly filled with pain, plant closings, and layoffs.

> *We had become marginalized by our Japanese competitors. There really was no viable option for us to work our way out. . . . The defining business of the company had not hit a pothole but an ultimate wall, and we had to make a very desperate move.*

The reality was that bad, and worse. (Grove later said that when it was all over, about one-third of the company had been shut down or laid off.) The process took three terrible years. As the company got out of the memory market, however, it put much of its resources into a new technology: microprocessors. While memory chips only stored memory, microprocessors were the *thinking* part of a computer—the part that actually performed calculations. Certainly, this new realm looked promising. But Grove admits that departing from his company's chipmaking past was one of the hardest decisions his management team ever made:

> *For us senior managers, it took the crisis of an economic cycle and the sight of unrelenting red ink before we could summon up the gumption needed to execute a dramatic departure from our past.*

By getting out of the memory business and focusing the company on the riskier microprocessor business, Grove was planting the seeds that would help the company grow into the mightiest in its new industry. A decade later, Grove would face a very different crisis that shared some elements with this first crisis. But before we turn to that other episode, let's sum up what can be learned from Grove's early experiences at Intel:

- **DEVELOP AN OUTSIDER'S PERSPECTIVE.** To truly study your organization—warts and all—look at your company as an outsider might. This is the perspective you need in order to make critical decisions. When Grove asked Moore what an outside CEO would do to deal with their crisis, he was applying this tenet to Intel— a kind of dispassion and detachment that ultimately saved the company and led it to even greater heights.

- NEVER INSULATE THE COMPANY SO MUCH THAT IT CAN-NOT BELIEVE IN ITS OWN UNDOING. Grove believes that a certain amount of paranoia is good for a company. Guard against incursions by competitors by keeping managers and employees on their toes. This does not mean paralyzing them with fear; rather, it means instilling a healthy amount of skepticism into the organization, so that everyone is focused on keeping the company on track.

STRATEGIC INFLECTION POINTS DEFINED: A 10X CHANGE

When Andy Grove arrived at his office one December morning in 1994, he had no idea that his world was about to be turned upside down once again. Intel was then in the midst of launching its latest-generation microprocessor, the Pentium processor. Some weeks earlier, a "minor design error" had been discovered in the chip, and reports of the problem began circulating online. However, the situation seemed to be under control, since testing showed that the problem was likely to occur only once in every 27,000 years of use.

But that fateful morning, everything changed. Grove was informed that IBM had stopped shipment of all Pentium-based computers. Intel's credibility—and, by extension, the entire company—was threatened as anxiety about the "bug" spun out of control in the business community. Grove faced a crucial decision: Try to reassure the world that the chip was sound, or replace every chip, which would cost Intel about *half a billion* dollars. He decided on the latter course of action. For the second time in a decade, the company was facing chaos, and possibly extinction. No matter what the outcome, Grove wrote later, nothing would ever be the same again:

> *Something has changed, something big, something significant, even if it's not entirely clear what that something is.*

What had happened? According to Grove, the rules that had governed his business for decades were no longer valid. Suddenly, what Intel thought—about quality, about reliability—*no longer mattered.* For the first time, computer *users,* who were not even Intel's direct customers, were demanding that an Intel product be replaced. Intel had reached what Grove calls a "strategic inflection point"—a point at which a company comes face to face with a massive change, one that is powerful enough to threaten the life of the enterprise.

Strategic inflection points, Grove later concluded, tend to arise following a long period of unbroken success. It is at these junctures, when the managers of the enterprise can't imagine anything but continued success, that the organization is most vulnerable. Grove has won wide acclaim for his seminal work on this topic, which was the main subject of his aforementioned book.

To Grove, the difference between ordinary change and a strategic inflection point (SIP) is the *magnitude* of the potential effect on the business:

> *We managers like to talk about change, so much that embracing change has become a cliché of management. But a strategic inflection*

point is not just any change. It compares to change the way Class VI
rapids on a river, the kind of deadly and turbulent rapids that even
professional rafters approach gingerly, compare to ordinary waters.

Grove even quantified a strategic inflection point by calling it a "10x change," meaning that the magnitude of the change is 10 times that of the changes that the business has been accustomed to. He noted that strategic inflection points are not restricted to technological changes. Almost anything can precipitate a strategic inflection point, including new or shifting competition, a change in regulation, a new channel of distribution, and so on. Strategic inflection points seldom announce themselves, and they can affect a single company or an entire industry.

The senior managers' earlier battle with the Japanese—and themselves—was a textbook strategic inflection point, and it had clarified Grove's thinking on the subject. What used to work now no longer works. Chaos, or at least a sense of being out of control, predominates. We had "lost our bearings," declared Grove. "We were wandering in the valley of death."

But as Grove had already discovered once—and was about to prove again—strategic inflection points don't necessarily mean institutional death. If managed skillfully, they can also breathe life into an organization.

STRATEGIC INFLECTIONS POINTS CAN STRENGTHEN ORGANIZATIONS

Not all strategic inflection points spell disaster for an organization and its managers. Says Grove:

Strategic inflection points offer promises as well as threats. It is at such times of fundamental change that the cliché "adapt or die" takes on its true meaning.

How can this be? Because companies that adapt in response to profound pressures often reinvent themselves, adding important new skills and competencies as they adjust to the external change. In most cases, *early detection of the strategic inflection point is key.* By acting before the potential damage inherent in the SIP occurs, organizations can not only fend off the near-term threat, but also develop an inner strength that can help them through difficult times for years to come:

Businesses are about creating change for other businesses. Competition is about creating change; technology is about creating change. . . . So the ability to recognize that the winds have shifted and to take appropriate action before you wreck your boat is crucial to the future of an enterprise.

As the organization approaches and comes to terms with an SIP, it's the corporate mind-set that counts. And, as stated earlier, *complacency* is the worst possible mind-set. It is much better to be fearful, says Grove, for fear keeps companies skeptical, sharp-edged, and on their toes. Therefore, when Grove was CEO at Intel, he worked to instill a healthy amount of paranoia into the organization, in the conviction that vigilance was one of the ingredients of the company's success:

I attribute Intel's ability to sustain success to being constantly on the alert for threats, either technological or competitive in nature.

The word paranoia is meant to suggest that attitude, an attitude that constantly looks over the horizon for threats to your success.

And *prompt action*, once vigilance has served its purpose, is equally important. Says Grove:

It is best when senior management recognizes and accepts the inevitability of a strategic inflection point early on and acts before the vitality of the business has been sapped by the "10x" forces affecting it.

DEALING WITH A STRATEGIC INFLECTION POINT: A MANAGER'S PRIMER

According to Grove, there are three warning signs that companies must heed in order to recognize a possible 10x force. Monitoring these signs may be an organization's best weapon against the sneak attack of a strategic inflection point.

1. YOUR KEY COMPETITOR IS ABOUT TO CHANGE. The organization that you have long viewed as your primary competitor may no longer be the one that you should fear most. This may be an early warning that things are being shaken up and that significant change is in the offing.

2. YOUR PRIMARY "COMPLEMENTOR" IS ABOUT TO CHANGE. The company that has long been your most important ally may no longer be as important—in the marketplace or to you. If something is happening that is changing the competitive position of a sup-

plier or strategic partner and that supplier or partner's importance to your company, it's possible that the same train is headed toward you.

3. MANAGEMENT'S ABILITY TO "GET IT" IS CHANGING. If members of the management team—including you—feel that they are out of touch with what is really going on out there, this is a clue that things out there may be changing at a faster rate than you anticipated.

PREPARING YOUR ORGANIZATION
FOR A STRATEGIC INFLECTION POINT

Obviously, the advent of a strategic inflection point is not under one's control. So what sort of actions does Grove recommend in order to ready the organization for such a massive change? First, says Grove, the CEO has to adopt and promote a "guardian" attitude:

The prime responsibility of a manager is to guard constantly against other people's attacks and to inculcate this guardian attitude in the people under his or her management.

So how can a CEO and other senior manager make sure that they are properly guarding against attacks? There are several ways:

1. LISTEN TO ALARMISTS. Grove calls them "helpful Cassandras"—those folks who are always proclaiming that the sky is falling. They are often middle man-

agers (for example, sales managers), who may be less focused on strategic issues, but are closer to the marketplace than most senior executives, and thus are in a better position to detect sea changes and paradigm shifts. Pay close attention to what they are saying, and encourage "Cassandra communications" from employees and managers the world over. Emails are a perfect medium for this kind of communication.

2. **ENCOURAGE RIGOROUS DISCUSSION AND DEBATE.** Only by thrashing out the possible implications of what appears to be a strategic inflection point—a debate that should involve different managers at several levels—can an organization determine whether it is truly facing a 10x change.

3. **EXAMINE—AND BE SKEPTICAL ABOUT—THE DATA.** There is often no substitute for cold, hard facts. But in making the call regarding a strategic inflection point, you may need to discount the data and put more faith in your instincts, since strategic inflection points are mostly about the *future*, which in all likelihood is not yet measurable.

There is a very definite progression of events involved in getting through a strategic inflection point, says Grove, who speaks from experience:

Getting through the strategic inflection point required enduring a period of confusion, experimentation, and chaos, followed by a period of single-minded determination to pursue a new direction toward an initially nebulous goal. It required listening to Cassandras, deliber-

*ately fostering debates and constantly articulating the new direction,
at first tentatively but more clearly with each repetition.*

LET CHAOS REIGN:
EXPERIMENT EARLY—AND OFTEN

Once you have identified a strategic inflection point, the
key to dealing with it effectively is to "let chaos reign," says
Grove. It is important for organizations to experiment in
multiple directions so that they have the power to respond
to a strategic inflection point. To put it in more dire terms,
if you're not already trying *all kinds of new things all of the
time*, it may be too late to start when the 10x change hits
you. So it is essential that you experiment constantly with
new products, new technologies, and so on:

*The dilemma is that you can't suddenly start experimenting when
you realize you're in trouble unless you've been experimenting all
along. It's too late to do things once things have changed your core
business. Ideally, you should have experimented with new products,
technologies, channels, promotions, and new customers all along.*

If an organization builds experimentation into its everyday business, it will have options available when a 10x
change occurs. This is particularly important now, Grove
asserts, as the Internet is emerging as *everybody's* strategic
inflection point.

When an SIP arises, it is up to management to choose a
clear path and take decisive action. This means (1) ex-
hibiting an unwavering commitment to righting the ship,
and (2) providing sufficient resources to accomplish that

end. Under Grove's leadership, as noted, Intel's "ship" was righted on more than one occasion, and the company returned the resources invested in it many times over. By the time Grove stepped down as CEO in 1998, Intel was a $26 billion juggernaut delivering more than $6 billion in annual profits.

Here are some historic examples of events that have presented a strategic inflection point to one or more industries:

- **THE INVENTION OF THE MASS-PRODUCED AUTOMOBILE.** When Henry Ford's first Model T rolled off his revolutionary "assembly line," it presented a strategic inflection point not only to the horse-and-buggy business, but also to the coach makers who were still making "horseless carriages" more or less by hand.

- **THE BIRTH OF AIR FLIGHT.** The Wright brothers' invention led to airmail and air travel, siphoning off first mail and later passengers from the railroads.

- **A NEW COMPETITOR.** Amazon.com went live in 1995, taking a significant bite out of the market share of traditional bricks-and-mortar bookstore chains like Barnes & Noble.

- **THE ARRIVAL OF ONLINE TRADING.** In the late 1990s, online brokers such as E★Trade and Ameritrade offered investors the chance to trade stocks at a fraction of the cost of traditional brokers like Merrill Lynch, turning the brokerage industry upside down.

What Would Andy Grove Do?

Returning to the case that opened the chapter, it should now be clear that your company was faced with a strategic inflection point when the supplement manufacturer started to steal market share. There are several similarities between this case and Intel's battle with the Japanese in the memory market in 1984. In both instances, the CEO underestimated the competition. None of the senior managers at Intel felt that the Japanese could marginalize Intel's memory business, and the same is true in this case. You didn't take the supplement manufacturer seriously, nor did you prepare the organization for the decline in its lead product.

So what do you do now? What would Andy Grove do? In this particular example, unfortunately, it may be a case of too little too late. Andy Grove would never have allowed the firm to become so vulnerable. He would have made sure that the company was experimenting with new types of drugs all along, keeping the drug pipeline full. He would have canvassed people lower down in the organization, knowing that the senior managers are often the last to know something. He would have listened to the "helpful Cassandras," who in your organization would have included the young researcher out of MIT. He would have encouraged vigorous debate, and he probably would not have dismissed the supplement alternative so quickly.

Had the company taken these measures, it would probably have more options than it does now. At this point, it appears almost too late to turn things around. Since your core business is fading, your only hope is to take the company in a new direction. Somehow, some way, you have to chart a new course for the company.

And there's always hope. Says Grove:

> When you are in a strategic transformation, you get kind of lost. Part of you wants to retreat back to doing what you know how to do, because it's familiar. . . . But your intellect tells you that's not really where you want to be. So you strike out in a new direction. . . . You have to feign more confidence than you feel, and you have to be convincing enough and courageous enough that you can affect the rest of the organization to follow you. You can course-correct as you go.

Most likely, your best chance of following Grove's model is to come up with a new drug or series of drugs that may prove to be your equivalent of the microprocessor. Keep in mind that Grove himself did not believe in the microprocessor in its early years. (In fact, he called it a nuisance.) If your firm has many "hooks in the water," perhaps it will come up with something that will turn things around. But discovery, development, refinement, and ultimate FDA approval take *years*, not months, and this will make it very difficult for your company to find its way out of the valley of death.

ASSESSING YOUR CEO QUOTIENT

1. How have you dealt with massive change? Do you and your employees roll with the punches?

2. Can you identify the last time you or your company encountered a 10x force? What happened? How well did your company cope with the change?

3. Do you feel that your organization is well positioned to detect the early warning signals of a strategic inflection point?

4. Has your organization developed an effective business strategy that combines a traditional bricks-and-mortar capability with an online component?

5. Do you make it a habit to listen to those Cassandras in your organization who are likely to identify a strategic inflection point before you do?

6. Does your organization routinely experiment with new products, processes, and technologies?

MORE LESSONS FROM THE CEO

1. **TO MAKE SURE THAT YOUR ORGANIZATION IS PREPARED FOR MASSIVE CHANGE, YOU MUST INSTILL A CULTURE THAT DESPISES COMPLACENCY.** Hold regular managers' meetings to discuss possible forces that threaten your organization, and encourage rigorous debate. Make sure that this debate filters down into the organization.

2. **TO ACHIEVE STEP 1, INSTILL A HEALTHY AMOUNT OF FEAR INTO THE ORGANIZATION.** Grove feels that this is key to making sure that complacency never infects your organization. Grove's embrace of paranoia may be off-putting to some, but it is difficult to argue with his results. Keeping everyone on their toes will

help the company sniff out new threats before those threats become insurmountable.

3. **MAKE SURE THAT MANAGERS THROUGHOUT THE WORLD CAN COMMUNICATE WITH YOU DIRECTLY.** (Email is probably the best way.) Remember that those managers who are closer to the customers are often aware of change before you are. It is imperative that you have a pipeline to those who are closer to the customer, so that you can get wind of any key shifts in your business context.

4. **MAKE EXPERIMENTATION WITH NEW PRODUCTS A REGULAR PART OF THE PRODUCT DEVELOPMENT PROCESS, EVEN IF THE REVENUES SEEM INSIGNIFICANT.** Remember that a new product at the right time may be what saves your company when it faces a massive threat. Had Intel not been experimenting with microprocessors, its prospects as it got out of the memory market—or stayed in that losing game—would have been very dim.

5. **IF APPROPRIATE TO YOUR INDUSTRY, MAKE SURE THAT YOUR COMPANY'S BUSINESS STRATEGY INCLUDES A UNIQUE ONLINE COMPONENT.** Grove regards the Internet as a strategic inflection point that *everyone* must face. Tomorrow's winners will be those companies that leverage the unique advantages of the Internet in a way their competitors have not yet thought of.

CHAPTER 6

Harness the Intellect of *Every* Employee

Smart people anywhere in the company should have the power to drive an initiative.

—BILL GATES, Chairman and chief software architect, Microsoft

The Internet is not just about new start-up companies. . . . The Internet is much more about existing businesses and how they take skills and customer base and move over to use these digital approaches to do things better. That's the most profound thing about this revolution.

—BILL GATES

What Would Bill Gates Do?

In the seat of the CEO: You are the newly hired CEO of a $75 million woodworking equipment manufacturer. You have extensive experience in the industry, and you've been hired to help spark productivity and growth. In the last 2 years, the company has grown by an anemic 3 percent annually, less than a third of the industry average, and productivity (as measured by revenue per employee) is also down significantly. Employee turnover is high, and morale is at an all-time low. The board feels that one of the key problems is the company's outdated computer system, and you've been hired to turn the company around.

As you take up the reins, you learn that much of the company's vital information has been either kept on paper or stored in antiquated computers that often malfunction. You speak to many employees who voice their frustration, and you then spend the next 6 months working with an outside contractor to update the entire system with new computers and to develop a new company intranet site.

Henceforth, the firm will eliminate a great deal of paperwork by digitizing its forms and increasing the amount of data that is input by customers. With the majority of company information online, there will be no more need to duplicate forms, purchase orders, etc. You estimate that the improved operating efficiencies will save the company close to $2 million within a year.

After announcing that the system will be ready within a week, you also let everyone know that a group of experts (the same outside contractor that designed the new systems and created the intranet site) will be hosting a week of orientation sessions. During these sessions, everyone from secretaries to senior executives will learn how to navigate the various components of the new system and use its applications.

The network administrator hosts the meetings and demonstrates how easy it is to access information and download key forms and data. On your instructions, she also explains which managers and employees will have access to what information (you have decided, against the advice of your contractor, that access should be limited by function, since turnover is high, and you don't want key information going to your competitors). She and her team will be available by phone on a day-to-day basis to answer technical questions. While they will not be able to answer specific questions about company data, her staff has been instructed to forward all communications to designated department leaders within the company.

A month after the system is up and running, it is evident, much to your shock and dismay, that the new system has *decreased* worker efficiency. How can this be? You assumed that the opposite would be true. Instead, you're finding that there is increased frustration, and that certain departments are getting bogged down in a bureaucratic nightmare.

For example, it takes days for sales managers to get key information from the marketing department, and the inventory managers are being deluged with questions from sales management. As a result, there is a backlog in orders, and the company is recording 20 percent fewer orders year over year than it did before the switchover.

Where did you go wrong? You brought in state-of-the-art systems, and you trained everyone to use them. How can productivity be *down*? More important, what should you do next?

What would Bill Gates do?

The story is now the stuff of legend. Bill Gates wrote his first software program as a young teenager. It was a program for playing tic-tac-toe on a computer. Years later, he and his long-time friend Paul Allen were hanging out at the Harvard Square newsstand and spotted the latest issue of *Popular Electronics*. On the cover was a picture of a build-it-yourself microcomputer kit called the Altair 8800. "This is our chance," said Allen to Gates.

Gates spent 5 weeks writing the BASIC program for the machine, and—sometime in the winter of 1975—the world's first microcomputer software company was born. "In time, we named it Microsoft," Gates later wrote. "Our initial insight made everything else a bit easier. We were in the right place at the right time. We got there first."

In 2002, Gates reflected on his initial vision:

> *The early dream was a machine that was easy to use, very reliable and very powerful. . . . We even talked back in 1975 about how we could make a machine that all of your reading and note taking would be done on that machine.*

Gates later secured his future when he snapped up the rights to an operating system, enhanced it, and sold the upgraded system to IBM. Microsoft's "disk operating system," known as DOS, helped propel the company into its position as the country's largest software company. Competitors who underestimated the barely-out-of-his-teens CEO did so at their own peril.

A quarter-century later, Microsoft is one of the world's largest and most powerful corporations. In 2002, Gates topped the *Forbes* 400 list of the world's wealthiest individuals, with a personal fortune of $43 billion. Some years earlier, Gates had handed the reins and the title of CEO over to Steve Ballmer, so that Gates would be free to help develop next-generation products (e.g., TVs, cell phones, tablet PCs) as Microsoft's "chief software architect."

During the economic and technology downturn of the early 2000s, Microsoft held up better than most technology companies, with a 12 percent increase in sales and an additional 5000 people added to the workforce in 2001 (while most of its competitors were cutting jobs). The company's signature Windows operating system still owns an eye-popping 93 percent of the market, but competitors in more than 20 countries have Microsoft in their crosshairs. In recent years, Gates and Microsoft have been forced to fight their fiercest battles in the courtroom rather than the marketplace, answering charges of monopolistic and unfair competitive practices.

Gates does not seem overly concerned, despite the fact that he has been ordered to publish 272 pieces of computer code for competitors. The next generation of Windows (nicknamed "Longhorn") is due out in 2005, and despite the long-drawn-out legal battles and a somewhat tarnished public image, Microsoft remains a company to be emulated. It is, above all, an *idea-driven* company. ("A computer in every home and on every desk," read an early mission statement.) Gates and his senior colleagues have spent a great deal of time thinking of ways to create an organization in which all employees can contribute to the knowledge base of the enterprise.

Of course, many companies *say* this is their goal. But Microsoft goes farther than most in *living* this goal. And, in part, as a result, Microsoft is one of the most valuable companies in the world, as well as one of the most profitable. In the fiscal year that ended in the summer of 2002, Microsoft's revenues topped $28 billion, and its net income approached the $8 billion mark—not bad for a Harvard dropout.

RETHINK THE WAY INFORMATION MOVES INSIDE THE COMPANY

Gates has been one of the main drivers of the technology revolution. Nevertheless, he has made some fundamental miscalculations about that revolution. For example, at first Gates was not a believer in the Internet, although he later came to view it as a powerful tool that would transform the very nature of work and commerce. As he explained in 1999,

> *It will allow people to collaborate across the globe. . . . It goes beyond just the idea of electronic commerce. It speaks to the very fundamental idea of how information moves both inside a company and between a company and its partners and customers.*

Gates views the Web as an information-sharing tool that can help to turn every employee into a knowledge worker. Some people believe that the largest changes caused by technology are behind us. Gates is not one of them. In the summer of 2002, he spoke of an upcoming "digital decade," because, he believes, the tools that will be created during the next 10 years will be the "best tools for empowerment and productivity the world has ever seen."

He explained how technology has influenced productivity:

The impact on productivity has been pretty phenomenal. If you just simply take the idea of Web browsing, e-mail, and the productivity software that's being used . . . that has had a very big impact. People like Alan Greenspan and others are looking at these numbers and saying it really is a fundamental change and far better than they would have expected going into those boom years.

As a result, Gates often speaks about a culture that encourages the entire workforce not only to think, but also to share their thoughts with coworkers and managers up and down the company hierarchy. In his book *Business @ the Speed of Thought,* the Microsoft founder used the phrase "digital nervous system" as a metaphor for information sharing within an organization.

He also comments frequently on the need for management to reevaluate its orientation toward information and on how making information readily available can help to fuel productivity:

The analogy to the value chain is a good one. Every worker, in a sense, is trying to add value, but your way of getting information to those workers—at meetings or via paper memos—we've taken as a given. Now that you can instantly provide all this information to these workers inside and outside your company, you get to rethink the way everything works.

Gates coined the phrase "digital nervous system" because he sees the role of digital information as analogous to the role of the central nervous system in the human body.

One of the primary benefits of a digital nervous system is that it synthesizes the collective intelligence of an organization. This comprises not only "big-picture" issues such as strategic planning, but also such mundane (but critical) activities such as interactions with customers. He also sees the Internet and the technology surrounding it as a way to better match buyers and sellers, which (as he argued in late 2000) was almost certainly what Adam Smith and his fellow inventors of capitalism had in mind in the first place:

> *Part of this process involves changing the way we buy and sell. A good reference point is to go back to Adam Smith. . . . He talked about the matching of buyers and sellers as being the fundamental mechanism of capitalism.*

Ultimately, a digital nervous system is about creating a faster, more decisive organization. Those companies that are better able to incorporate all of their information into an integrated system, and make all that knowledge accessible to all employees, are the ones that will have the fastest reflexes, and will react most quickly to the lightning-paced changes in the marketplace.

In order to create an organization closer to Gates's ideal, consider taking the following step (if your organization has not done so already):

- DIGITIZE THE COMPANY'S MOST VITAL INFORMATION. As the rest of this chapter will underscore, it is impossible to create a true digital nervous system unless the company's most important information is made available in a digital format. Make sure that key sales reports, memos, initiatives, and so on are available online. Also make sure that they are readily accessible to all the employees and managers who need them.

THE RISE OF THE INTERNET
AND THE END OF MICROSOFT?

The story of how Microsoft reacted to the Internet phenomenon illustrates the way Gates empowers workers by encouraging communication at every level of the hierarchy—and thereby derives great benefit. Had Gates taken a different tack, Microsoft might have become a very different company. The story begins in the mid-1990s. While some companies were gearing up for the Internet in a big way, at that time Microsoft was a laggard. By the fall of 1995, Microsoft—long accustomed to the status of media darling—was being derided for not responding to the Internet quickly or effectively enough.

In retrospect, Gates readily admits that he simply missed the boat at first. Within a few years, however, Microsoft had reversed course in dramatic fashion. The company acquired or made investments in dozens of Web-based companies, and went from a company without an Internet strategy to a company *obsessed* with the power of this new technology:

> If we go out of business, it won't be because we're not focused on the Internet. It'll be because we're too focused on the Internet.

In other words, once the software giant grasped the importance of the Internet, it responded with urgency. So how did a huge company like Microsoft go from "not getting it" to being one of the key players in the industry? For one thing, Gates listened to employees who had their ears closer to the street than he did, and were hearing the new ideas that he was not hearing.

FOSTER A CULTURE IN WHICH IDEAS RULE

While Microsoft clearly was not oblivious to the Internet in the early to mid-1990s, it did not put the Internet high on its priority list. (Gates recalls that he ranked the Internet as number five or six on his priority list back then.) What is most compelling about Microsoft's shift to an Internet strategy is that it did not originate with Gates or another senior manager. Instead, the firestorm of change was sparked by an employee.

During a trip to a college campus, a Microsoft employee noticed that Cornell University was using the Internet for far more than just computer-science applications. Upon his return to the company, he composed and fired off a "the-sky-is-falling" memo, declaring that Microsoft would "go out of business" unless it listened to him. Eventually, the memo made its way to Gates, where it had an enormous impact:

> *Microsoft's awareness that something very dramatic was going on around the Internet really came from employee[s] . . . so he became a change agent at Microsoft. . . . And people looked at that, they looked at the other memos they had saying similar things, and we said, boy, this is profound.*

Two observations: First, it took some guts for Gates to make this admission. (Wasn't he the resident visionary?)

And second, this type of bottom-up strategic initiative would have been impossible in a company with an inflexible hierarchy. But Gates was both appropriately humble and flexible. He took those messages very seriously, and he organized several company retreats in 1994 and 1995 to respond to them. By the end of 1995, the company had a new top priority, and the Internet was defining the future of the company. Gates credits the company's use of electronic mail—and a supportive company culture—with fostering an environment in which ideas could trump hierarchy:

> *If we hadn't had electronic mail, and the type of culture that that creates . . . there's no doubt that our leadership would have been eclipsed if we had taken that long to really get it, and drive Internet standards into our products. So for us this digital approach has made the difference between being on top of things or actually falling behind.*

Here are several ways to ensure that your organization emphasizes ideas and intellect sharing:

- **MAKE SURE THAT THE ORGANIZATION HAS AN INFRA-STRUCTURE AND CULTURE THAT FOSTER IDEAS FROM EVERYONE.** Gates credits the culture of Microsoft with helping to spark its Internet strategy. Unless employees are genuinely encouraged to contribute their thoughts and ideas, organizations risk missing out on potentially critical information.

- **CONSIDER HOSTING COMPANY RETREATS TO FOCUS ON KEY INITIATIVES AND TO HELP THE MANAGEMENT TEAM CORRECT ITS COURSE.** Once Gates realized that the Internet would indeed be a breakout technology, he hosted several key retreats in order to devise a cohesive strategy for the company. Retreats or multiday meetings on an important initiative can help an organization redefine its focus.

EMPOWER WORKERS WITH INFORMATION THEY CAN ACT ON

Gates leads by example, inviting anyone in the organization to send him an email at any time. And he doesn't want just the good news—he wants bad news even faster (another Gates principle is, "Bad news must travel fast"). In today's fast-changing business environment, anyone, anywhere, can get a paradigm-busting idea, and organizations that do not listen to all employees—particularly those who are closest to the customers—risk being overtaken by more nimble competitors:

> *Smart people anywhere in the company should have the power to drive an initiative. It's an obvious, commonsense policy for Information Age companies, where all the knowledge workers should be part of setting the strategy.*

Management's willingness to listen to everyone in the company is only the first step. If employees are to have "the power to drive an initiative," they need far more than email. If they are to contribute to the maximum possible extent, today's employees need access to all sorts of information: sales reports and data, customer information, market analysis, the latest product instructions, and so on.

Giving the workforce easy access to all this information was nearly impossible before the Internet, but today, there is almost no excuse for organizations not to provide this information to their employees. Gates feels that this shift to a knowledge-based economy will make many of the "old-economy" jobs obsolete, and he argues that every worker is potentially a knowledge worker. Armed with all of this "instant knowledge," workers can (and must) do more than ever before:

> You very quickly start to get the knowledge workers more empowered and, in turn, get more value out of them. You can redefine customer service; you can redefine how you plan products and get lots more input and feedback along the way; you can respond more quickly when you perceive the marketplace telling you to do something.

Gates describes the transformation of old-economy clerical workers into more sophisticated value contributors as "shifting knowledge workers into higher-level thinking." It's the middle managers and employees, says Gates, who need accurate data the most, since they're the ones who are doing so much of the work. Gates urges companies to abandon their habit of hoarding information, and instead to teach their employees how to interpret, analyze, and act on that information.

Gates is convinced, however, that there is still much to be done in this area. While e-commerce is a reality for most corporations, its applications are often far too limited. In practice, he concludes, most organizations do not take advantage of the full potential of e-commerce. "In any meaningful sense, it has not happened," he declared in the spring of 2002.

In other words, e-commerce has not lived up to its potential. In part, this is because there is a great deal of inefficiency in sharing information, particularly between companies. As an example, Gates describes two companies that are engaged in an e-commerce transaction. If you examine the knowledge workers and systems in one company and the knowledge workers and corresponding systems in the other, you find mismatches and resulting inefficiencies.

Why? Because, according to Gates, few companies engage in purely digital transactions. In fact, the digital part of the transaction (in this case, a purchase order) is often only a minor aspect of the transaction. Gates says that in reality, workers are supplementing the digital part of the transaction with phone calls and faxes and emails, then updating systems to reflect the results:

Actually, there's more effort spent in just impedance, moving the information around, than there is in the real work itself; that is, the work of designing the products or doing good customer service.

Here are several ideas for improving your organization's information flow:

- ENCOURAGE ANY EMPLOYEE OR CUSTOMER TO CONTACT YOU DIRECTLY VIA EMAIL. The truth is that in most large companies, no one would dare send an email to the CEO, particularly one delivering bad news. (Someone—either an intermediate supervisor or the CEO him- or herself—would be likely to shoot the messenger.) These companies are likely to be left behind in the digital revolution.

- AIM FOR "PURE" DIGITAL TRANSACTIONS. Gates argues that there is still a great deal of inefficiency in most organizations' transactions. This is because there are few purely digital transactions. Encourage collaboration among your customers, your suppliers, and the key internal departments (especially IT) to work toward pure digitization of transactions (such as order fulfillment).

DEVELOP YOUR CORPORATE MEMORY

Another key is ensuring that a company retains, and can quickly retrieve, the information that it accumulates. Gates calls this "corporate memory." And it isn't only employees who need access to vital information; customers, too, should have access to this information. This way, account managers and customers can refer to the same document when discussing an account or a billing issue. In the same spirit, all customer interactions should also be documented.

Think of all this as a complete digital archive that will allow employees and customers to locate a form or record in seconds. Gates also feels that most companies (including Microsoft) have too many forms, and he suggests that companies eliminate as many as possible. He also recommends that companies put all forms online and encourage feedback from users. Gates has a litmus test that helps companies evaluate their progress in this vital area:

> *Your corporate memory is not very good unless somebody who is working on a project can sit down at their PC and in less than 60 seconds call up any memos or documents that might relate to a sim-*

ilar project that was done in the past. If it takes more time than that, people probably won't go and find it. So in that sense, your corporate memory is not an asset.

Here are some ways to improve your organization's corporate memory:

- MAKE SURE THAT YOUR CUSTOMERS AND SUPPLIERS HAVE THE SAME ACCESS TO INFORMATION AS YOUR EMPLOYEES. This will make all transactions that much easier. Such an approach may require a radical shift in mind-set, as well as a realignment of the ways in which your organization interfaces with key constituencies.

- MAKE SURE THAT IT TAKES NO MORE THAN 60 SECONDS TO RETRIEVE ANY DOCUMENT OR FILE. If your organization cannot pass this test, the digitization of all those transactions and forms is of little use.

What Would Bill Gates Do?

Returning to the case of the frustrated woodworking company CEO, it is apparent that you went wrong when you instructed the outside contractor to allow only limited access to information. By restricting access to information by *function,* you created functional silos within the company and made a mess of the entire system. When sales managers and salespeople have to ask which products are in stock, you know you have a big problem.

Bill Gates would know that information can't be restricted by function. In order for information to flow properly within a digital nervous system, all employees—and suppliers and customers as well—must have access to all relevant company information. Anything less than that will hamper productivity and slow things down. Your outside contractor knew that and advised you against restricting access to information. Your concern about employees leaving and taking information with them helped to undercut the entire system. Was your concern well placed? Perhaps. Did your decision to restrict access to information cost more than the alternative? Probably.

The good news is that you can fix things rather easily by making all information available to all departments. If you think about it, there is actually very little information that your competitors could learn that would hurt you. You can go one step further by inviting key suppliers and customers in and training them as well, and giving them access to relevant forms and screens. By doing so, you can create a far more efficient and capable organization, reduce frustration, and boost morale.

ASSESSING YOUR CEO QUOTIENT

1. Does your organization still have old-economy jobs in which employees do little more than enter information into a system?

2. Do you (and other managers) encourage employees at all levels and locations to send an email to anyone, including the company chairperson, at any time?

3. When was the last time you made an important strategic decision based on an idea or recommenda-

tion made by someone *not* on your senior management team?

4. Are all of your company's key reports (sales, customers, incentive plans) available by some electronic means?

5. Do all of the employees who need access to those key reports have access? Do the customers have access to those same reports?

6. How good is your organization's corporate memory? Can an employee or customer find a particular record online in less than 60 seconds?

MORE LESSONS OF THE CEOS

1. MAKE SURE THAT EVERY REPORT—AND EVERY OTHER VITAL DOCUMENT—GENERATED BY YOUR COMPANY IS AVAILABLE IN A DIGITAL FORMAT.

2. SET UP A MEETING WITH YOUR DIRECT REPORTS TO REINFORCE YOUR COMMITMENT TO CREATING AN EFFICIENT, FULLY FUNCTIONING DIGITAL NERVOUS SYSTEM. Make sure that your managers know that your goal is to create a knowledge-based organization in which the vast majority of essential information is available online.

3. ESTABLISH A TASK FORCE TO DEVELOP YOUR ORGANIZATION'S CORPORATE MEMORY. Be sure that all key de-

partments are represented (manufacturing, marketing, sales, etc.). Lead the first meeting yourself, and establish the goals and a timeline for developing a fully functioning digital nervous system.

4. **FROM THE VERY START, MAKE SURE THAT CUSTOMERS ARE PLACED AT THE CENTER OF THE ENTIRE EFFORT.** Constantly remind everyone in the organization that one of the primary goals of a digital nervous system is to improve customer service at every level.

5. **IN KEEPING WITH THE SPIRIT OF THE DIGITAL NERVOUS SYSTEM, LET EVERYONE KNOW HOW COMMITTED YOU ARE TO FAST COMMUNICATION AT EVERY LEVEL.** Get in the habit of sending out companywide emails on a regular basis, keeping everyone informed on important initiatives. Make it clear that you welcome feedback and suggestions (both good news and, especially, bad news) from every employee, regardless of level and location. This may create discomfort among some managers, so be prepared to deal with the accompanying fallout. This may mean making other meaningful changes to gradually alter the company culture (e.g., holding meetings with small groups to discuss new priorities and initiatives).

CHAPTER 7

Create a Performance-Driven Culture

The rule at Southwest is, if somebody has an idea, you read it quickly and you respond instantaneously. You may say no, but you give a lot of reasons why you're saying no, or you may say we're going to experiment with it in the field, see if it works.

—HERB KELLEHER, Founder and former Chairman,
Southwest Airlines

We try to value each person individually at Southwest and be cognizant of them as human beings—not just people who work for our company. What we're really trying to say is, "we value you as people apart from the fact that you work here." That approach has been very helpful to Southwest.

—HERB KELLEHER

What Would Herb Kelleher Do?

In the seat of the CEO: You are the CEO of a successful $25 million chain of steak houses that is well known throughout the United States and Europe. The restaurant chain has built its reputation on its excellent food and unconventional service. Waiters and the bus staff sing to customers, or perform poetry and movie "readings." Even the chefs come out of the kitchen and get into the act. This is no accident, of course: Your company's training program teaches all employees and managers to do just about anything to delight your customers.

You are now in the process of hiring a key senior manager for your flagship restaurant in Chicago. Several of your managers have interviewed more than 200 candidates, and they have narrowed the field to three, all of whom seem highly qualified. You have a file on each, and you bring each in for a final interview:

Bill S. He seems to have what it takes to be a good manager. He attended a top-notch hotel/restaurant school and has a strong résumé. Most of his 14 years in the business have been with one of your smaller competitors— a highly profitable outfit in the Midwest. When asked what he is most proud of, he speaks of how he helped turn that company around. The company was in trouble, with razor-thin margins and few growth prospects. Thanks to his financial management, cost cutting, and other innovations—he developed new processes that allowed the company to seat more customers per restaurant—the company became a leader in its niche. He concludes his interview by telling you that the last ad campaign was his idea ("Great food at a great price, and the fastest service in town"), and by speaking of the importance of building a strong team and a family-like culture.

Sally J. She has been in the restaurant business for just under 8 years. Her last position was in an upscale seafood restaurant in New York. She appears passionate about her work, and her enthusiasm is contagious. When asked why she left her last job, she declared that she could no longer tolerate management's arrogance toward employees and customers. ("They acted as if the customer should be grateful for getting a seat in the restaurant," she explained.) She speaks modestly of her accomplishments, but she also admits that she has made some mistakes during her career (e.g., as manager of the New York restaurant, she sometimes alienated management by challenging its ideas). She also has limited understanding of financial management, which is important in the new position.

Harry P. He is the most seasoned of all of the candidates, with two decades of experience, most recently in New Orleans. Harry attended one of the best hotel/restaurant programs in the country, and he says that there is no job that he could not handle. Once he starts talking about his achievements, he goes on for some time, speaking of the "groundbreaking" things he accomplished in previous jobs. He is most proud of what he achieved in his last job, at a Bourbon Street bistro, where profits increased by more than 20 percent even though the restaurant was serving 5 percent fewer customers.

So those are the three candidates. Whom do you hire? Why? Is there a clear choice? What are the factors that will shape your decision?

What would Herb Kelleher do?

Let's face it, there aren't many chain-smoking, tattooed CEOs leading *Fortune* 500 companies. But former Southwest Airlines CEO Herb Kelleher is not your typical chief executive. Southwest was founded over cocktails at the St. Anthony's Club, a San Antonio watering hole, in 1966. The idea for the airline was groundbreaking: a budget airline that would fly between Dallas, San Antonio, and Houston. Almost from day one, the company played the role of a scrappy kid fighting off the village bullies. The day after Southwest got its approval to fly, for example, angry competitors petitioned the court for a restraining order to stop it.

The battle went all the way to the Supreme Court, where Kelleher and Southwest got the last laugh. Competitors Braniff and Texas International were indicted for conspiring to put Southwest out of business.

Kelleher took on the role of CEO later, when the company had only 27 planes and was doing $270 million in business. By 2001, the company had 30,000 employees and was a $5.7 billion business. In the fall of 2002, Southwest's market capitalization was 10 times that of American and United combined. Even though the feisty lawyer-turned-airline-chairman handed over the CEO reins in 2001, much of the company today remains the organization he created.

KELLEHER ON CULTURE:
AN IRREPLACEABLE ASSET

Southwest has defied the conventional wisdom on everything from its pricing structure to its no-assigned-seats policy. But this remarkable carrier—the only major airline that has never had a money-losing year—has garnered its greatest accolades for its unique corporate culture. Its employees are incredibly loyal, and they have described the atmosphere of Southwest as more akin to that of a small family than of a large company. Kelleher has always hated bureaucracy and the glacial pace of decision making that goes with it. He is convinced that Southwest's culture and people are its greatest assets:

> *The culture of Southwest is probably its major competitive advantage. The intangibles are more important than the tangibles because you can always imitate the tangibles; you can buy the airplane, you can rent the ticket counter space. But the hardest thing for someone to emulate is the spirit of your people.*

Kelleher has firsthand knowledge of how culture drives profits. Kelleher's workforce constantly delivers. One example is its performance in early 2000, when Southwest faced a crisis. Fuel costs had tripled, threatening the company's bottom line. In a heartfelt letter, Kelleher asked every employee to find a way to save the company just $5 a day. If they were successful, the company would save over $50 million a year, the chairman explained. Employees jumped to answer the call. One group of mechanics found a way to heat planes for less money. Another department volunteered to do its own janitorial work. In the first 6 weeks, Kelleher's dedicated employees saved the company more than $2 million. It was a clear demonstration of what is possible when there is real trust between management and workers:

Thinking like a small company isn't just another flavor-of-the-month management philosophy; it's a way of life that has been deeply embedded into the culture from day one.

HIRE FOR CULTURE

All of Southwest's corporate policies and practices send a consistent message: "We are a serious airline and a formidable competitor, but we will have fun while earning a profit." From their very first interviews, prospective employees are immersed in the company's offbeat behavior. In some interviews, for example, groups of pilots are asked to swap their suits and ties for Southwest Bermuda shorts. (Only those who comply are considered.) On average, only 4 percent of the 90,000 people who apply for work at Southwest each year are hired. In other words, Southwest is harder to get into than Harvard—all the more surprising when one considers that Southwest is a budget airline.

But the tight funnel doesn't screen out the fun lovers. In fact, they have a clear leg up. Pilots crack jokes over the intercom, contradicting the ultraserious stereotype of airline travel. The point of all the jokes? To make sure that passengers are treated to a great experience. Southwest "hires attitudes," says Kelleher. It does not believe in "leading by numbers," and it believes that "intangibles are more important than tangibles":

Our esprit de corps is the core of our success. That's most difficult for a competitor to imitate. They can [buy] all the physical things. The thing you can't buy is dedication, devotion, loyalty—feeling you are participating in a cause or a crusade.

In order to make sure that there is a proper fit between employee and company, Southwest looks for people who share its unique mix of enthusiasm, affinity for people, and off-center sense of humor. To do that, the company uses a personality test that ranks candidates—everyone from pilots to mechanics—on seven traits: cheerfulness, optimism, decision-making ability, team spirit, communication, self-confidence, and self-starter skills (score less than a 3 and you're out). Kelleher says that Southwest is no place for inflexible, rigid people:

> *If you're an altruistic, outgoing person who likes to serve others and enjoys working with a team, we want you. If you're the kind of person who enjoys a more secure, more regimented, more inflexible, more rule-governed type of environment, that doesn't mean you're a bad person, but we're probably incompatible. We shouldn't even get engaged, much less married.*

Based on Kelleher's advice, here are two ideas that might help when your organization is interviewing candidates for an important position:

- **VALUE THE INTANGIBLES.** Kelleher understands that intangibles are often more important than tangibles. Attitude, for example, is impossible to measure, but it has proved a huge factor in creating the culture at Southwest Airlines.

- DEVELOP YOUR OWN LIST OF HIRING CRITERIA. As discussed, Southwest rates applicants on seven criteria (cheerfulness, optimism, decision-making ability, team spirit, communication, self-confidence, and self-starter skills). Make a list of the traits that are most important to you and your organization, and make sure that candidates measure up in terms of those characteristics before making them a job offer.

KELLEHER ON PROFIT: "A BY-PRODUCT OF CUSTOMER SERVICE"

Southwest is a company that is rich in paradox—a large company with a small-company spirit. What does that mean? While many companies take themselves very seriously, Kelleher is saying that it's perfectly acceptable to lighten up, even when you're working—no, Kelleher would say, *especially* when you're working. Kelleher believes that CEOs need to spend more time with their external and internal customers, informally as well as formally, and fulfill the other requirements of their jobs at night and on weekends. The former Southwest leader estimates that he spent roughly half of his time as CEO with employees and customers. In those sessions, formal and informal, Kelleher urged his employees not to concern themselves with numbers, but instead to focus on *service*:

We tell our people, "Don't worry about profit. Think about customer service." Profit is a by-product of customer service. It's not an end, in and of itself. It's something that's produced by your efforts and the way that you treat each other and the way you treat the outside world.

A Wall Street analyst once asked the Southwest chief if he was afraid that he was losing control of the organization. Kelleher responded with his usual brand of candor: "I've never had control, and I never wanted it." The CEO went on to explain that in a true environment of participation, managers don't need control:

If you create an environment where the people truly participate, you don't need control. They know what needs to be done, and they do it. And the more that people will devote themselves to your cause on a voluntary basis, a willing basis, the fewer hierarchies and control mechanisms you need.

KELLEHER ON A LEADERSHIP CULTURE

Kelleher feels strongly about his two primary constituencies—employees and customers. In correspondence (at least with this author), Kelleher uses a capital C and a capital E when writing about Customers and Employees. This CEO is serious about putting these two groups in a class by themselves.

To Kelleher, *culture* means taking care of the people that the business depends on every day:

I think that even very hardheaded "managers" (we don't like the "manager" word) might be influenced to focus more on the importance of "culture" if they understood that fun, enthusiasm for the job, and concern for the well-being of each other were not only the key to joyful productivity and pride, but also the intangible quality that is most difficult for a competitor to emulate successfully.

When asked if he feels that the issue of culture is often overlooked in times of stress—for example, in the heat of a merger or acquisition—Kelleher responded with a resounding yes. He asserted that cultural issues are often subordinated when the pressure is on. And this, he emphasized, is a critical mistake, because many mergers that fail hit the rocks because of a clash of cultures:

Culture clash contributes to many of the failures of such combinations, and their incompatible cultures produce internal tribal warfare.

KELLEHER ON COMPENSATION: PAY EXECUTIVES *LESS* AND EMPLOYEES *MORE*

Southwest has achieved some extraordinary things in the area of employee relationships. Its pilots, for example, agreed to freeze their salaries for 5 years, taking their chances with stock options instead. When another employee group, which had effectively voted itself out of a union a few years earlier, began feeling vulnerable, Kelleher responded by issuing a personal contract—signed by Kelleher himself—to each of those employees.

These unconventional practices would be impossible without a foundation of trust and fairness. Kelleher says that his brand of culture would not be possible without a fair compensation system up and down the organization.

He says that while he pays employees above-average salaries, he pays officers *less* than their counterparts at competing carriers:

> *Our officers (whom I consider the best in the business) are paid 30 percent less, on average, than their counterparts. . . . On the other hand, most of our employees are at or above average pay levels in our industry. We try to make up that difference to our officers with stock options, but of course that depends on how well the company does.*

The company also allows all employees to participate in a generous profit-sharing plan. Kelleher feels that giving employees a stake in the company is smart business and helps boost productivity. And there is ample evidence that these unconventional compensation practices work: Southwest is the fourth-largest airline in America (a $6 billion organization that has achieved three consecutive decades of profit). It flies 50 million passengers per year, and it has won the coveted "Triple Crown" (best monthly on-time record, best baggage handling, and fewest customer complaints) an unparalleled 32 times.

LIMIT STRUCTURE TO FOUR
MANAGEMENT LAYERS

How does structure fit into Kelleher's vision of a large company with a small-company spirit? Obviously, it isn't enough just to hire the right people, give them profit sharing, and have them crack jokes or pop out of overhead bins. In order to make sure that decision making does not get bogged down, the Southwest chairman insists on a maximum of four layers of management between the CEO and front-line supervisors. Kelleher's goal is to push responsibility down into the field as much as possible, so that people feel free to make decisions. The workers who perform best in Kelleher's company are self-starters who are confident enough to make their own decisions:

> *We've tried to create an environment where people are able to, in effect, bypass even the fairly lean structures that we have so that they don't have to convene a meeting of the sages in order to get something done. In many cases, they can just go ahead and do it on their own. . . . Our leanness requires people to be comfortable in making their own decisions and undertaking their own efforts.*

Despite its success, Southwest has had its share of skeptics over the years, particularly on Wall Street. Most analysts agreed with Kelleher that Southwest's secret was its small, family-like culture. But many also believed that the culture could not survive if the company got too large. However, Southwest has succeeded in maintaining its culture while achieving meaningful growth (with close to 30,000 employees, and counting). Much of the credit belongs to CEO Kelleher, who steadfastly stuck to his original vision of the company:

> *The bigger you get, the harder you must continually fight back the bureaucracy and preserve the entrepreneurial spirit. . . . You've got to keep that spirit alive within the company, no matter how big it gets.*

KELLEHER'S STEPS TO A
HIGH-PERFORMANCE CULTURE

When asked in 2002 what advice he would give to other companies attempting to instill the "Kelleher spirit" into their own organizations, the Southwest founder took the question very seriously. His response (sent in written form to this author) is nothing less than a culture-enhancing blueprint for other managers and organizations to emulate. It is reproduced here with virtually no editing (in other words, this is Kelleher, "uncut"):

Bureaucracy is antithetical to accomplishment. Success in most businesses depends upon the quick achievement of external results, rather than the purity and institutionalization of internal processes. For those businesses wishing to become more entrepreneurial and less bureaucratic in nature, I would recommend at least the following steps:

1. *FOCUS UPON THE WORLD OF COMPETITORS, CUSTOMERS, AND SOCIETAL CHANGES, rather than upon an inside general office world, sometimes composed primarily of slavish devotion to forms, protocols and procedures.*

2. *DON'T BE AN ONION, BE AN ORANGE. Reduce layers from "bottom" (there is none—just "us") to "top" (there is none—just "us").*

3. *REDUCE, TO THE MAXIMUM EXTENT POSSIBLE, THE NUMBER OF PERMANENT CORPORATE COMMITTEES. Use ad hoc groups to solve particular problems; include people on them who actually perform the functions involved (Cus-*

tomer Service Agents, Mechanics, etc.), and then dissolve those groups when the problem is solved.

4. *THERE IS NO "PERFECT KNOWLEDGE," THERE IS ONLY GOOD JUDGMENT.* Don't waste an inordinate amount of time on analyzing, studying, discussing, and planning (i.e., avoiding the risk of making a decision). Set deadlines on decision making—"at this meeting, within two weeks, etc."

5. *REQUIRE YOUR OFFICERS AND OTHER "MANAGERIAL" PERSONNEL TO SPEND TIME ACTUALLY WORKING WITH (NOT WATCHING) EMPLOYEES AND EXTERNAL CUSTOMERS in the field and to report on what they did, what they learned, and what they intend to do with their acquired knowledge.*

6. *RECOGNIZE THAT ALL PAPERS PRODUCED, INCLUD-ING THE BUDGET, ARE SIMPLY WHITE PAGES WITH LITTLE BLACK MARKS ON THEM;* they are impotent un-less they lead to meaningful action or decisive (not inadvertent) inaction, and they are not immutable.

7. *ESCHEW INFLEXIBLE RULES AND PONDEROUS MAN-UALS DESIGNED TO REGULATE THE MINUTIAE OF CORPORATE LIFE AND CUSTOMER INTERACTION, and* instead, rely upon a well-understood and accepted set of corpo-rate values. . . .

8. *BE A TRUE "INTELLECTUAL":* Value ideas on their merits, rather than on the status, relationship, or credentials of those who submit them, and invite everyone to submit those ideas directly to the top (there is none—just "us").

9. *GIVE "MANAGEMENT" PERSONNEL PROBLEMS TO SOLVE IN AREAS OTHER THAN THOSE OF DIRECT RESPONSIBILITY and give Employees the opportunity to learn others' jobs; learning, empathy, and unity are most often the results.*

10. *FOCUS UPON THE ESSENCE, NOT THE PERIPHERAL— e.g., this is the issue that confronts us; this is how we are going to resolve it; and now tell me how we are going to overcome (not succumb to) any impediments that might frustrate our proposed resolution.*

11. *HAVE A GENERAL STRATEGIC PLAN, NOT A LONG-RANGE PLAN OR GUIDELINE, as to what you are and what you aspire to be in the world that confronts you; use that strategic plan as a benchmark, not a bible, with respect to your decisions and actions; and then move nimbly and quickly within the ambit of that plan.*

12. *IN ORDER TO HAVE A DEFINABLE AND UNDERSTANDABLE "NICHE," you must be prepared to eschew a revenue-generating opportunity and give up market segments.*

13. *BE HUMBLE; BE APPROACHABLE; BE ETHICAL; LEAD BY SERVING; DON'T BE PERSONALLY GREEDY; don't discriminate; be fair; be firm, but never mean; have fun; enjoy people; tolerate mistakes; take risks; and share sacrifices.*

14. *ALWAYS REMEMBER THE G.O. (THE SUPPLY CORPS) IS THERE TO SERVE PEOPLE AT THE FRONT LINES, NOT THE REVERSE.*

Kelleher also added specific ideas for managing the "people part" of the business—and, more specifically, concrete suggestions for developing a culture and ensuring that bureaucracy doesn't work *against* that culture (which he deems to be the company's greatest asset).

Once you have established an appropriate G.O. culture, recognize that your company's Employees are your premier Customers: Hire, train, infuse, involve, and inspire them, and they will be tolerant, empathetic, welcoming, caring, good humored, and altruistic toward each other and your external Customers.

1. *HIRE GOOD ATTITUDES IN PREFERENCE TO BAD ATTITUDES (EVEN OVER BAD ATTITUDES WITH SUPERIOR DEGREES, EXPERIENCE, AND EXPERTISE).*

2. *TRAIN PEOPLE IN TWO THINGS: LEADERSHIP AND CUSTOMER SERVICE.*

3. *HAVE A CUSTOMER (INTERNAL AND EXTERNAL) REPRESENTATIVE AT YOUR HIGHEST OFFICER LEVEL WHO IS KEPT INFORMED OF ALL DELIBERATIONS AND PROPOSALS ON ALL SUBJECTS AFFECTING YOUR INTERNAL AND EXTERNAL CUSTOMERS (from benefits to methods of operation to work hour schedules to plans for company parties, etc.)*

4. *LET YOUR PEOPLE BE THEMSELVES AT WORK, manifest their true personalities, and not have to put on a "work mask" or worry about the niceties of hierarchical protocol.*

5. *CELEBRATE THE ACHIEVEMENTS OF YOUR PEOPLE, OFTEN AND SPONTANEOUSLY;* celebrate the milestones in your people's personal lives, such as weddings, marriages, birthdays and births, holidays, and more; care for, and grieve with, your people when they are ill, lose loved ones, experience catastrophes, or have other unhappy events in their lives. In short, value your Employees as people, not just workers.

6. *CLEARLY DELINEATE WHAT YOUR COMPANY IS DOING AND WHY;* make every Employee a participant, not an onlooker; ennoble the purpose of the work that's being done (you're not simply processing passengers, you're giving Americans the Freedom to Fly and thereby making a valuable contribution to society).

7. *ADDRESS EMPLOYEE CONCERNS INDIVIDUALLY, PROMPTLY, AND SPECIFICALLY;* even a "mental problem" is still "a problem" for the person involved.

8. *THROUGH ROLE MODELS, CELEBRATIONS, AND COMMUNICATIONS, HONOR EXCELLENCE IN SPIRIT AS WELL AS PERFORMANCE;* generate pride in accomplishment and selflessness; and remember that the intangibles, which can't be easily emulated, are more important than the tangibles, which can be purchased.

9. *TITLE AND POSITION ARE UNIMPORTANT; LEADERSHIP QUALITIES ARE ALL-IMPORTANT;* and everyone, no matter the title or position, is a leader by example. Correspondingly, it is an injustice to your people not to change poor leadership.

10. *COMMUNICATION FROM THE HEART IS MORE IMPOR-TANT THAN COMMUNICATION FROM THE HEAD, AND INFORMAL COMMUNICATION IS JUST AS IMPORTANT AS FORMAL COMMUNICATION (e.g., "It's a pleasure to see you." "I was delighted to hear about your new baby." "Did you find that hat in a trash can?" "I hear your music recital went beautifully!"). Moreover, communicating goals, ideas, emotions, inspiration, and love is just as important as communicating facts and figures.*

11. *IF YOU ARE NOT ON FIRE ABOUT WHAT YOU'RE DOING, WHY YOU'RE DOING IT, AND THE PEOPLE WHO DO IT WITH YOU, THEN YOU CAN'T KINDLE THEIR MINDS, HEARTS, AND DEVOTION TO A CAUSE.*

What Would Herb Kelleher Do?

Picking up from the scenario at the beginning of the chapter (the three candidates seeking the management job), which one did you decide to hire? Which one would Kelleher have selected? Let's begin with the candidates that the ex-Southwest chairman probably would have *eliminated*.

He would have eliminated our first candidate, Bill S., because Bill spent much of the interview taking credit for the company's success (e.g., he turned the company around, he came up with the last successful ad campaign). That would be anathema to Kelleher, who feels that humility, selflessness, and modesty are indispensable attributes for any employee. Although he mentioned a small-company culture at the end, it seemed as if it was an afterthought.

He would also have decided against the third candidate, Harry P., who seemed far more interested in numbers and profits than in customer service. As long as profits were up, he was not concerned that the restaurant he managed served 5 percent fewer customers. Kelleher says, "Don't worry about profit. Think about customer service. Profit is a by-product of customer service. It's not an end, in and of itself."

This, of course, leaves Sally J., the candidate that Herb Kelleher would most likely have selected. Sally was the most modest, speaking of her mistakes as well as her successes. Yet she maintained an infectious enthusiasm and a genuine passion for her work. She left her last job because management did not seem concerned enough about satisfying customers—a stance that Kelleher would respect. Although she was the least experienced of the three, Kelleher, who strongly urges managers to "hire for attitude," would have been impressed enough with Sally to hire her. He feels that resumes and experience are not as important as finding managers who fit the company's unique culture.

ASSESSING YOUR CEO QUOTIENT

1. In order to figure out how your culture stacks up, perform the following quick, nonscientific "culture audit." For each question, rate your company's performance on a scale of 1 to 5 (5 means strongly agree, 1 means strongly disagree).

   a. In our organization, there is a high degree of trust between the workforce and management.

   b. Workers in our company are dedicated, and often go beyond the call of duty to accomplish an important task.

    c. Most workers feel free to make decisions without approvals from their boss(es).

    d. Most workers feel that they have a stake in the company, financial or otherwise (e.g., profit sharing).

    e. We hire for attitude, making sure that a person's personal qualities are weighed along with her or his credentials.

2. Think about the core values that exist in your organization. Are they the right ones? Are they well known throughout all levels of the company? Are they constantly communicated to employees?

3. Are there no more than four layers of management between the CEO and your front-line supervisors?

4. Are the employees of your company empowered to make important decisions, or are they forced to obtain several layers of approvals in order to do so?

5. Think about the way your company hires its people. Does your organization hire for attitude, or more on "straight" credentials?

MORE LESSONS FROM THE CEO

1. IF YOU SCORED 3 OR LESS IN MORE THAN HALF OF THE QUESTIONS IN THE AUDIT, YOU MAY NEED TO MAKE SOME MEANINGFUL CHANGES IN YOUR COMPANY'S CULTURE. Consider putting together a culture task force (in-

cluding employees at different levels) to make rec-
ommendations to management on how the company can become less bureaucratic and more
participative. The simple act of involving workers
will help morale and will show that management is
serious about improving things.

3. WORKING WITH OTHER MANAGERS AND THE CULTURE
TASK FORCE, PINPOINT THOSE PROCESSES AND PROCE-
DURES THAT WOULD BENEFIT MOST FROM A "PROCESS
FACELIFT." Remember that the goal is to reduce lay-
ers of approvals and red tape so that processes are
streamlined.

4. THE FINAL OUTPUT OF THE CULTURE TASK FORCE
SHOULD BE A CULTURE PLAN THAT INCLUDES ACTION
ITEMS FOR MAKING THE COMPANY LESS BUREAUCRATIC
AND HIERARCHICAL. The plan should be presented to
senior managers, and decisions as to which ideas are
to be implemented should be made on the spot.

5. TAKE MEANINGFUL STEPS TO ELIMINATE LAYERS OF
MANAGEMENT OVER A PERIOD OF TIME. If there are
more than four layers of management between the
CEO and your front-line supervisors, decision making will most likely be slowed down. This will probably require planning for a reorganization within the
next 12 months.

6. ONCE YOU HAVE A PLAN IN HAND, MAKE SURE THAT IT
GETS COMMUNICATED THROUGHOUT EVERY LEVEL OF

THE ORGANIZATION (e.g., via speeches, managers' meetings, companywide emails, newsletters, etc.).

7. **DON'T UNDERESTIMATE THE IMPORTANCE OF MAKING THE WORKPLACE AN ENJOYABLE EXPERIENCE.** Take a page from Herb Kelleher's management book and let employees know that you are committed to making the workplace an enjoyable experience. Remember that motivated employees are far more likely to serve your customers well.

CHAPTER 8

Learn from Competitors, but Remain Faithful to the Vision

There is only one boss. The customer. And he can fire everybody in the company from the chairman on down, simply by spending his money somewhere else.

—SAM WALTON

Most everything I've done I've copied from someone else.
—SAM WALTON

What Would Sam Walton Do?

In the seat of the CEO: You are the founder and CEO of a small, $8 million publishing company that produces short "how-to" manuals for the weekend woodworking set. You started the company almost a decade ago, after searching unsuccessfully for books to help you with your weekend projects (everything from wooden bird feeders to sleds for the kids). Once you realized that there were few books on woodworking projects out there (at least, few of the kind you were looking for), you decided to leave your publishing job and start your own publishing company. It had always been your dream to run your own business, and you figured that surely there were plenty of other people who shared your passion for woodworking and would buy your products.

Today, your dream is a reality, although you're far from a typical publisher. Unlike most other how-to books, yours are not sold in bookstores. Instead, they are sold in hobby stores and through some national home-improvement chains. While these chains don't usually carry books, your unique format—88-page, highly designed books that lie flat thanks to a special binding—have strong visual appeal. Just as important, you promised your distributors that you would not price the books above $10 (they are priced at $7.95 to $9.95), and that the distributors could retain 20 percent of the purchase price of every book they sold. Again, this was a winning proposition.

Thanks to a strong "push" from your distribution channels and an equally strong "pull" from readers, the series caught on immediately. It seemed that the weekend warriors could not get enough of them.

Today you have more than 100 woodworking project books on your list, and you decide to hire an editor-in-chief to assume responsibility for day-to-day product development. His job is to sign authors to write books for the company, figure out what to publish, and grow the business. This won't be easy, as you see it, since you've already covered just about every woodworking topic you can imagine. After a lengthy review of the options, the new editor-in-chief comes to you with several ideas to change the business and make it more profitable.

His first idea is to expand some of the best-selling books (perhaps up to 150 pages) and raise their retail price to $12.95. (You have never raised prices.) He also proposes expanding the distribution of your line to include traditional bookstores (such as the national chains). Finally, he recommends that the company grow via acquisition, by buying a small cookbook publisher that is up for sale. While the price of the cookbook company seems reasonable, you know nothing about cookbooks; however, your editor-in-chief published several successful cookbooks in his first publishing job almost 20 years ago, and he says that he has great confidence in his ability to manage this new business successfully.

How do you feel about your editor-in-chief's plans? Which parts do you agree to? Do you take the plunge into the cookbook market? Or do you find another way to grow the company? What do you do?

What would Sam Walton do?

Even the quickest glance at the 2002 *Forbes* list of the 400 wealthiest individuals is likely to reveal a startling fact: Five of the wealthiest people in the world share the same last name. This is because they are related—by marriage or birth—to one of the greatest entrepreneurs of the twentieth century—a folksy merchandiser who loved to compete by taking on huge competitors. He was what one American president called "an American original," and his unique rags-to-riches story is the stuff of legend.

His name, of course, was Sam Walton.

Born in Kingfisher, Oklahoma, Thomas Walton was a farmer, banker, and farm-loan appraiser who did not believe in taking on debt. The secret to success, Thomas told his children, was "work, work, work." His son Sam learned that lesson well. As a child, he also got his first taste of retailing—on the customer's side of the counter when family holidays included visits to local stores.

Sam Walton kept visiting stores for the rest of his life, long after he opened his own first store (in 1945). It was a wise practice, since the fast-moving retail industry threatened to leave behind those who failed to spot trends and adapt to them. Walton did not get left behind. He was constantly tinkering with his products and his presentation. And although his early stores were successful, Walton did not hesitate to make a radical change in his retail formula. In 1962—the same year in which Kmart, Woolco, and Target got their starts—Walton opened his first Wal-Mart store. Discounting was then sweeping across America, and Walton wanted his piece of this new retailing phenomenon.

Former Wal-Mart CEO David Glass, who worked with Walton for many years, remembers him as someone who was driven "to improve something every day." This was more than a philosophical stance; it was a practical necessity: His first stores simply were not as good as those of his competitors. "At the start," Walton later admitted, "we were so amateurish, and so far behind." Over the next four decades, though, the company founded by Sam Walton would become not only the world's largest retailer, but also the world's largest *company*. (In 2002, Wal-Mart topped the list of *Fortune* 500 companies.)

How did he do it? According to Glass, "Sam's philosophies were really pretty basic, pretty simple, pretty straightforward—which is probably why they worked as well as they did."

A PIONEER OF THE LEARNING CULTURE

Sam Walton got into retailing by accident. Upon graduating from college, he started as a J. C. Penney management trainee at $75 per month. Later, he borrowed the money he needed to open his first store: a Ben Franklin 5-and-10 franchise in Newport, Arkansas. One of his competitors there was Sterling, a store that was doing twice as much business as the Ben Franklin, even though it was smaller than Walton's store. Walton responded by spending a great deal of time in the Sterling store, studying its displays, comparing prices, and generally annoying its owner.

One of the realities Walton faced was that all Ben Franklin franchise owners were expected to buy at least 80 percent of their stores' goods from Butler Brothers, the company that franchised Federated Stores and the Ben Franklin stores. These goods didn't come cheap, given the 25 percent markup that Butler charged its franchisees. Walton, infuriated by what he saw as an extortionate margin, attempted to go directly to local and regional manufacturers to buy his goods. But most of them turned him down, fearing Butler Brothers' wrath. So Walton went farther afield, traveling as far as Missouri and Tennessee to buy goods as cheaply as possible. This allowed him to cut his costs, pass those savings on to consumers, and increase his sales volume.

Five years later he lost the lease to his store—a setback that he later called the low point of his business life. Undeterred, he relocated and opened his second store. These early stores looked very little like today's Wal-Marts. Instead, they were classic "variety stores," characterized by high levels of customer service, with clerks helping customers select items that ranged from cleaning supplies to cookware to cosmetics.

But in the early 1960s, a new self-service retail model began to catch fire in different parts of the country. When Walton got wind of it, he rode a bus all night to see a self-service store for himself. He was immediately won over, and he set out to copy and improve upon this new model.

His wife of half a century, Helen, described one of her husband's most important work habits in Walton's memoir, *Made in America*: "What really drove Sam was that competition across the street . . . always. Looking at his prices, looking at his displays, looking at what was going on. He was always looking for a way to do a better job."

This is a key piece of the Walton saga: While Walton was indeed an original, many of his best ideas were not. From his earliest days in business, young Sam Walton raced around, notebook in hand, learning from competitors and bringing the best ideas into his stores. He spread that attitude around the company during his Saturday morning meetings with managers. Walton was quick to admit, for example, that he did not create the concept of discounting, and he was equally ready to admit that that he borrowed almost all of his best ideas from competitors:

> *Most everything I've done I've copied from someone else. . . . I probably visited more headquarters offices of more discounters than anybody else—ever. . . . I'd ask lots of questions about pricing and distribution, whatever. I learned a lot that way.*

When it came to learning, nothing was off-limits to Walton. He studied competitors' prices, displays, merchandising techniques, and so on, in order to improve his own stores. He was able to spot a diamond in the rough—a rare skill that David Glass emphasizes: "Most of the best ideas came from our competitor's stores. It's often been said that he [Walton] spent more time in competitors' stores than they did. In a lot of cases, that's true. But I have gone through stores with him many times, thousands of times where the competitors' stores . . . would look really bad . . . almost God awful. But he would never say that. He would always find some good idea in there, and everybody, of course, picked up on that."

Walton was also a pioneer of the belief that those closest to the customers have the most to teach the company—an idea that would not gain currency for many years. Recalls Glass, "He genuinely believed that all of the best ideas came from the bottom up, not from the top down, and particularly that all those people who interfaced with the customer knew more about the business and more about what we needed to do and more about how to improve it than anyone else."

Walton said, "In the whole Wal-Mart scheme of things, the most important contact ever made is between the associate in the store and the customer."

Here are some ideas taken from Walton's playbook that you can incorporate into your own:

- NEVER STOP LEARNING—FROM COMPETITORS, CUSTOMERS, AND YOUR OWN EMPLOYEES. That's how Walton refined his strategy and improved his stores. He spent most of his time in stores, learning from everyone around him.

- ASSUME THAT THERE IS SOMETHING YOU CAN LEARN FROM EVEN YOUR "WORST" COMPETITORS. There is something worthwhile that you can learn from *every* competitor. He was always looking for at least one good idea to bring back to his own business. His managers picked up on that, and followed Walton's lead.

- CONSIDER WEEKEND MEETINGS WITH MANAGERS TO GET A JUMP ON THE COMPETITION. Choosing Saturday mornings to meet with his managers to discuss strategy and incorporate what they had learned into the business was one of Walton's best competitive moves. Walton said that it was in those meetings that the company first decided to try things that seemed unattainable. Those meetings were pivotal, because they were the vehicle Walton used to make his "corrections"—2 days before the competition had a chance to catch up.

INNOVATE, EXPERIMENT, CREATE ANARCHY

As stated earlier, Walton founded Wal-Mart not out of some grand vision of reinventing the retailing world, but to avoid being run over by a new breed of competitor. Although Walton had never operated a "pure" discount store before founding Wal-Mart, he had learned many lessons about how the game was played, including the paradoxical nature of discounting: *Lower* prices lead to *higher* profits.

He knew, in other words, that if he charged $1.00 for an item rather than $1.20, he would sell three times as many units. The higher volume and revenue more than made up for the reduced profit margin, leading to an increase in overall profits. Walton often experimented with different items and prices, and felt that his constant tinkering was a key success factor:

> *I could never leave well enough alone, and, in fact, I think my constant fiddling and meddling with the status quo may have been one of my biggest contributions. . . . I have always been driven to buck the system, to innovate, to take things beyond where they've been. . . . I have always been a maverick who enjoys shaking things up and creating a little anarchy.*

Here are some additional Walton lessons that are worth incorporating into your own business:

- CONSIDER LOWERING YOUR PRICES TO BOOST YOUR VOLUME. Think about experimenting with lower prices, particularly during rough economic times. Of course, your ability to do this will depend on the price elasticity of your industry and your product niche. During economic downturns, buyers are more price-sensitive than ever. The lower prices may very well increase sales enough to offset the lower margins.

- **DON'T BE AFRAID TO SHAKE THINGS UP.** Walton said he liked to create "a little anarchy." Try that at your own organization. For example, consider giving some of your best people new and unexpected assignments or challenges. Ask them to come up with a new product idea, or an idea for making the organization more productive or streamlined. Or, if your department or unit seems particularly complacent, consider moving people around so that they have new challenges.

FAITHFUL TO THE VISION: LOWEST PRICES

Walton received early confirmation that he had a winning formula: It soon became clear that customer loyalty to a given retailer was mostly fiction. Customers would shop almost *anywhere* if the prices were lower.

An amusing episode at the time of the opening of the second Wal-Mart store confirmed the wisdom of Walton's new approach. Wal-Mart was opening a store in Harrison, Arkansas, not far from the local (and relatively "upscale") Sterling store. In those days, store openings were big events. Kids got free donkey rides, and patrons were offered free watermelon in the parking lot. But this particular store opening was a disaster almost from the start. The scorching heat had two unexpected consequences: exploding watermelons and what might euphemistically be called "excitable" donkeys. As a result, the parking lot turned into a slippery, smelly mess, which made its way into the store on customers' shoes.

Nevertheless, shoppers came, browsed, and purchased. They bypassed the tonier store up the street, ignored the mess on the floor, and *bought.* Walton knew then that low prices were the key to his business. Even though he made many mistakes in those first years, Walton felt that his vision kept the company on the right track:

> *What we were obsessed with was keeping our prices below everybody else's. . . . We managed to sell our merchandise as low as we possibly could, and that kept us right side up for the first ten years—that and consistently improving our sales in these smaller markets by building up our relationship with the customers. The idea was simple: when customers thought of Wal-Mart, they should think of low prices and satisfaction guaranteed.*

Walton's obsession with low prices helped fuel the company's incredible growth and helped him to leapfrog his competitors. This was a good thing, because despite Walton's zest for learning, in Wal-Mart's early years the company was very much a David up against many Goliaths. Five years after starting Wal-Mart, for example, Walton had only five stores, each bringing in less than $10 million in revenues annually. In sharp contrast, Kmart had 250 stores with total sales of $800 million.

But Walton had patience, and he had the courage of his convictions. He believed that he could win in the long run because many discounters never fully committed to the discounting model, which calls for low prices across the board:

It's amazing that our competitors didn't catch on to us quicker and try to stop us. . . . What happened was that they really didn't commit to discounting. They held on to their old variety store concepts too long. They were so accustomed to getting their 45 percent markup, they never let go. With our low costs, our low expense structures, and our low prices, we were ending an era in the heartland. We shut the door on variety thinking.

Some retailers, such as Sears, failed to acknowledge that Wal-Mart was one of their key competitors. The result was good for Wal-Mart and bad for Sears. Walton knew that stores that had near-monopolies in their geographic area—even discount stores—tended to charge what they thought the market would bear. This almost always meant that their goods cost more than the equivalent products at the local Wal-Mart. The result was predictable. By 1980, Wal-Mart had more than 275 stores doing over $1 billion in sales. By 1990, Wal-Mart had over 1500 stores, and sales had topped $26 billion. The formula, rigorously applied, was magic.

Here are several take-aways from the Walton model that may work in your business:

- ONCE YOU HAVE THE "FORMULA" FOR YOUR INDUSTRY, WORK ON IMPROVING IT. Walton knew that having the lowest prices was the key to winning the discounting game. Once he had established that, he set out to improve on that model with an increasingly sophisticated store-location strategy (discussed in the next section), better merchandising tactics, and ever-lower prices (by buying in incredible bulk, eliminating middlemen, and working closely with suppliers to get every possible price break).

- **STAY FAITHFUL TO THE VISION.** Walton knew that the key to the company's future was never to break with the company's guiding principle: *low prices*. Even if there was no other discount store within 100 miles, he made sure that every Wal-Mart stayed true to the vision. This helped him to maintain his customer base even after new competitors entered his "neighborhood."

WALTON'S SMALL-TOWN STRATEGY

One of the critical ingredients in Wal-Mart's success was Walton's selection of store locations. Walton made the decision to place Wal-Marts in small-town America, even in places where the population appeared to be too small to support the store. Other large discounters, such as Kmart, believed that a trade territory of 50,000 people was the minimum required to support a discount store. Walton built his first store in Rogers, a town of 8000. The small-town strategy was established early, and definitively, when Walton's wife, Helen, refused to live in any town with more than 10,000 people. Luck and accident play their part in business success, and Wal-Mart is no exception to this rule. Out of Helen Walton's personal preference grew a strategy that—at least for the time being—proved farsighted:

> *We could really do something with our key strategy, which was simply to put good-sized discount stores into little one-horse towns which*

everybody else was ignoring. . . . When people want to simplify the Wal-Mart story, that's usually how they sum up the secret of our success: "Oh, they went into small towns when nobody else would."

It seems clear that Wal-Mart's small-town strategy gave the company an early edge, giving it an opportunity to refine its methods before tackling more competitive markets. Eventually, however, the small-town strategy began to work to the company's disadvantage. In an interview in the fall of 2002, former Wal-Mart CEO David Glass explained that in many cases, the most difficult discount store to run is one that has *no* competition. "It is much easier to be successful if you have a pretty good competitor or more than one competitor," said Glass. "If you have no competition in a small town, they have nothing to compare you with. . . . One of the great misconceptions about Wal-Mart is that in the early days we succeeded in the small towns because of an absence of competition. Exactly the opposite is the case. The reason he [Walton] was able to explode in growth in this company was because there was very intense competition in the towns we went to."

Experts such as Northwestern University marketing professor Philip Kotler believe that Wal-Mart's small-town strategy was ingenious, but had other consequences that can't be overlooked in assessing the company: "The fact is, he killed all the mom-and-pops that made up those little town centers, and there was no one else doing that. Kmart was not an issue at that time; they were big, but they were in the city areas. . . . Consumers loved him because he really lowered their costs of buying things. But it's the businesspeople who died in the process."

David Glass vehemently denies that Wal-Mart killed the small stores. "There are far more small businesses that go out of business in towns where there is not a Wal-Mart," he argues, "than where there is." He asserts that the small businesses' real problem was that, "They didn't change with the times. . . . They wanted to open at 8:00 and close at 5:00. . . . They didn't want to be open on weekends, because they wanted weekends off and would never ask themselves the question, when does my customer want to shop. . . . It's just like dirt roads going away. . . . It's just an evolution of America."

What can managers take away from Walton's growth strategy? Although few companies have Wal-Mart's size advantage, there are lessons that can be applied in other business situations:

- **DON'T BUILD WHERE THEY ARE, BUILD WHERE THEY ARE GOING TO BE.** Walton's early strategy of building Wal-Marts where there were no other stores made great sense. By building stores and waiting for the population to grow out to him, he was building for the future. Think of ways to apply that lesson to your business by creating products or entering markets that might still be a year or two from fully developing. That leads to a second, closely related idea.

- **BE FIRST TO MARKET.** In the towns where he built his early stores, Walton's location strategy ensured that he was the first to market. Companies that are first to market with a new product or service often reap substantial rewards. Of course, being first is easier said than done. One way to try to anticipate future needs is to incorporate a "first to market" mind-set into your planning and training. Consider assigning one of your key managers the task of leading a small team charged with coming up with one or two product ideas that might pay dividends for the future.

A KEY TO DOUBLE-DIGIT GROWTH: STAY PRODUCT-DRIVEN

While store location and low prices were part of Walton's model, so too was the concept of merchandising. Deep down, Sam Walton thought of himself as a merchant first. "In Wal-Mart stores they don't want many brands," explains Philip Kotler, confirming Walton's strong instincts for merchandising. "Basically, Wal-Mart features only a few brands, where they get good volume discounts, and so on. What makes them work is the *breadth*—every category is represented—but it's *not* depth within a category. That's different from stores that feel that they have to have all five or six brands that might be around."

Wal-Mart's merchandising strategy was formed early on and changed little over the years. Walton loved to buy an incredible amount of one item—say, Tide detergent—and make it hugely visible in his stores. He would build a gigantic display of it, hang it from the ceiling, or whatever. Walton felt that his competitors failed when they lost their merchandising instincts:

If you are going to show the kind of double-digit comparable store sales increases that we show every year, and grow a company the way we've grown ours, you have to be merchandise driven. I can name you a lot of retailers who were originally merchandise driven, but somehow lost it over the years.

Remember that Walton had two decades of retailing experience before he founded Wal-Mart. He had routinely bought unusual items and sold them by the carload. He perfected the art at Wal-Mart, buying items at rock-bottom prices and selling them by the planeload. In many cases, the more off-the-wall the item, the better it sold, and Walton made stars out of off-beat items, such as Moon Pies or Bedmates, arranged in colossal displays all over the store.

THE FIRST INFORMATION-AGE CEO?

The tremendous growth of Wal-Mart can be attributed to more than store location and Moon Pies. In fact, a key part of the Wal-Mart story is how the company won the information technology race. Although he needed some convincing at first, Walton soon grasped the importance of harnessing information technology in order to cut costs and create a genuine competitive advantage. In fact, *Time* magazine made the case that Walton may have been "the first information age CEO."

As early as 1983, Wal-Mart pioneered the application of new systems, including the use of satellite technology, that enabled the company to get incredible amounts of data flowing between stores, warehouses, and the home office in Bentonville, Arkansas. The satellites were the key, Walton wrote, because once the system was in place, they had all sorts of vital information "pouring into Bentonville over phone lines."

The scale of this effort is staggering. In the late 1980s, for example, Walton had a 135,000-square-foot building constructed just to house Wal-Mart's sophisticated computer system. By 1992, the company had spent $700 million on its information systems, amassing one of the largest such systems in the world (second only to that of the Pentagon). The key to the technology, of course, was not how much was spent, but how the company *used* this new resource. Walton said that the faster people got information, the faster they would use it. Useful applications emerged almost immediately. For example, the huge flow of data played a pivotal role in helping the company work more closely with its suppliers. Armed with all that data, the company was better positioned to use its inventory knowledge to cement working relationships with key manufacturers.

In 2002, Philip Kotler assessed the relative sophistication of Wal-Mart's use of information technology and the role of that technology in inventory management: "Some people call Wal-Mart an information company, and that's not an exaggeration. They are so advanced in their information systems. They know every night how many Pampers have sold that day, and they get Procter & Gamble, through this alliance they have worked out, to ship enough Pampers on a daily basis to make up for what was sold . . . . What this really means is that Wal-Mart's secret is inventory management. They don't believe in stock, they believe in flow. And they have a thing called 'cross-stocking.' Cross-stocking means that it doesn't actually get stored into the warehouse. . . . The big truck comes and brings stuff that is . . . unloaded into the smaller trucks, that then go out and to where it is put onto the shelf."

Of course, it is in the interest of suppliers to forge these

close relationships. Procter & Gamble has an office in Bentonville, Arkansas, with 150 employees that is devoted to a
single brand of toothpaste. According to David Glass, Wal-
Mart was the first company to transform the supplier relationship from an adversarial one to something more akin to
a partnership. Once the philosophy of "supplier as partner"
was established, Wal-Mart's systems became an even more
powerful tool that helped the company become more efficient and cost-effective. As Glass puts it, "We used to go
through a spiel that we'd say to the supplier, we're not
really your customer. The consumer is your customer.
We're only a conduit to get your merchandise to them. So
if you believe that, then the right thing to do is say, all
right, let's look at the whole thing from the time you man-
ufacture the goods until the consumer carries them out of
the store, and what's the most efficient way to do it. And
what we found was that they could eliminate a lot of costs
that they built into their business to protect their interests
against us, and we could eliminate costs and do things more
efficiently. . . . If you form this partnership and it works,
then you can really revolutionize the business."

By almost any measure, Wal-Mart did indeed revolutionize the business. In late 2002, Wal-Mart was the largest
civilian employer in the world, with more than 1.2 million
associates worldwide (23 percent of them outside of the
United States). In addition, Wal-Mart was responsible for a
substantial percentage of the total U.S. retailing market and
more than 1 percent of America's gross domestic product.

And Wal-Mart's accomplishments go well beyond scope
and scale. The company has actually changed the way we
live. The *New York Times*, citing a study that was conducted
by the McKinsey Global Institute, concluded: "By making

goods cheap and available, Wal-Mart has raised the standard of living of average Americans." Not bad for a small-town retailer who got into the business because he didn't want to be run over by his competitors.

What Would Sam Walton Do?

Returning to the case of the editor-in-chief with the novel ideas for expanding your business, what should you do? While there is not necessarily one answer to this particular scenario, chances are that Sam Walton would have rejected *all* of his editor-in-chief's ideas. All of them are a departure from the original vision of the company, and there are better ways to grow the company than by tinkering with the success model or acquiring a business that you know nothing about. Let's take a closer look at the ideas.

First, Sam Walton would not have broken his word by raising the prices of the books. If he had vowed not to raise the price of the books above $10, he would never break his promise or let down his customers—particularly in the realm of keeping prices down!

As for distributing the books via bookstores, this is a more complex question. In fact, unless you knew that retail bookstores have 100 percent return privileges, you would not have had all the information you needed to figure this one out. But Walton would have asked a thousand questions before deciding on this, and he would almost certainly have decided not to go the traditional bookstore route. First, he would have learned that bookstores usually receive close to a 50 percent profit margin on books like his, not the more attractive 20 percent that he gave his existing distributors. (Also, the book's format would not lend itself very well to traditional store shelves.) Lastly, if the retail bookstores couldn't sell the books, they could return them and get all of their money back! That could create a big inventory problem for his small company.

As for buying a cookbook company, he would probably avoid that as well. Cookbooks are not woodworking books, and this alternative would not capitalize on any of the company's strengths (e.g., your ability to do the graphics, your knowledge of woodworking, your existing customer base and distribution system). The cookbook market is crowded, and your editor-in-chief hasn't published one in 20 years! This is a very difficult market for a small company to penetrate. Sam would have wrestled with those issues before making any company acquisition.

Better growth ideas include woodworking books for kids (projects that parents could work on with their children) and project books on crafts other than woodworking, such as working with clay or ceramics. This would be closer to the original vision of the company.

ASSESSING YOUR CEO QUOTIENT

1. Does your organization have a well-articulated vision? Is that vision commonly known and understood throughout the company?

2. Can you honestly say that you spend time each week learning what your competitors are up to?

3. Do you routinely scrutinize your primary competitors' practices? (This could mean not only checking them out with a personal visit, but also spending time studying their offerings, their promotions, etc.)

4. Think about the lessons you have picked up from studying your competitors. Have you incorporated these lessons into your own business? Have you improved on them?

5. How would you describe your relationships with your key suppliers? If you do not think of them as genuine partners, then there may be ways to improve those relationships—and, by extension, your business.

MORE LESSONS FROM THE CEO

1. MAKE SURE THAT THE COMPANY HAS A CLEAR VISION STATEMENT, AND THAT IT GETS COMMUNICATED THROUGHOUT THE COMPANY. Walton's vision was known by just about every Wal-Mart associate throughout the company. It is critical that employees and managers know the vision.

2. ALLOCATE A CERTAIN AMOUNT OF TIME EACH AND EVERY WEEK TO STUDY WHAT YOUR COMPETITORS ARE DOING, AS WELL AS STUDY ANY OTHER BUSINESS THAT MIGHT YIELD GOOD IDEAS. Studying competitors was vintage Walton. He never stopped learning from them, and he attributed his best ideas to rivals.

Make it a habit to write down the best ideas you glean from the competition and to share those ideas with your colleagues and direct reports. Figure out how those ideas can help your business.

3. **WORKING WITH THE IDEAS YOU HAVE WRITTEN DOWN, FIGURE OUT WAYS IN WHICH YOU CAN BUILD ON THEM TO COME UP WITH SOMETHING FRESH AND NEW.** Enlist others in your organization to work with you to build on the knowledge culled from the marketplace. Remember that Walton learned something from every store he walked into—even the "godawful" ones.

4. **MAKE SURE YOUR INFORMATION SYSTEMS ENABLE YOU AND YOUR ORGANIZATION TO OPERATE AT MAXIMUM EFFICIENCY.** Even though Walton was not a true believer at first, he eventually realized that the faster he and his managers received good information, the faster they could put it to good use.

5. **HIRE FOR ATTITUDE, NOT NECESSARILY EXPERIENCE.** While Walton did not underestimate the importance of experience, he searched for employees who shared his zest for business. If you are given the choice of two job applicants with reasonably similar qualifications, hire the one with the best attitude, even if he or she has less directly relevant experience.

ACKNOWLEDGMENTS

In researching and writing this book, I was fortunate enough to secure the cooperation of several key CEOs and business experts, whose assistance and insights helped make this a richer book.

Let me begin by acknowledging the CEOs (and former CEOs) who took time out of their busy lives to respond to this author's list of queries. Although he was mapping out his own memoir at the time, an unselfish Lou Gerstner went to great lengths to patiently answer each question regarding his turnaround of IBM (in a 6-page document). In his answers were many valuable insights that helped to unlock some of the mystery surrounding his turnaround of the deeply troubled computer maker. He proved that in the long run, attitude and culture are as important to organizations as balance sheets and income statements. I am grateful to him for his thoughtful analysis.

Michael Dell also agreed to be interviewed, and provided a wealth of information on how a customer-centered organization is created and maintained. He showed how an organization could gain market share in even the worst of economic times, even when so many technology firms were going off of a cliff. He demonstrated that delivering superior customer value could provide the greatest competitive advantage of all.

I also wish to acknowledge Herb Kelleher, who scribed a lengthy response to a set of questions aimed at getting inside the mind and methods of the man that founded the world's most profitable airline. The former CEO of Southwest Airlines answered my queries in writing, a lengthy document that included his rules for running a large organization. Since he has not written his own book, I am in his debt for contributing his original ideas to this work.

I also wish to give special thanks to Northwestern's Phil Kotler. Dr. Kotler was gracious enough to grant me an extensive interview regarding the CEOs in this book. He also contributed several new ideas while challenging my thinking in several key areas. I am grateful to him for taking the time to assist this author in his pursuit of the leadership threads of the best CEOs.

I would like to thank the individuals who reviewed the manuscript and provided valuable insights: Dr. Joe Goldblatt, Dean of the M. Shawn Feinstein School of Business at Johnson and Wales University, and Harvey Thompson, a former Global Practice leader at IBM. Thanks also to Denny Cummings of the Chicago Union League Club for his assistance and encouragement. I also express my gratitude to Jeffrey L. Cruikshank, for taking his pen to this work, once again enriching a book by applying just the right touch.

My wife, Nancy, merits a singular note of acknowledgment. She showed infinite patience over the almost four years this project developed. She read so many different drafts she likely lost count, always offering helpful advice and guidance along the way. She is a talented individual and a wonderful partner, and I offer thanks every day for having her by my side.

I would also like to acknowledge the efforts of the talented team at McGraw-Hill. My editor, Philip Ruppel, made the type of suggestions that only he could, helping to keep the manuscript on track from its earliest rendition to the final draft. Thanks also to Lynda Luppino, Anthony Sarchiapone, and David Dell'Acio for his creative cover design. Lydia Rinaldi, publicity manager, always brings great enthusiasm to each project, and I am grateful to her for her fine efforts. Peter McCurdy, production manager, has again shown that he can manage details expertly, turning ideas and the written word into a first rate product. I also offer my gratitude to Chitra Bopardikar, Amanda Yee, and Allyson Arias, for her dedication and hard work from Florida to Frankfurt.

Lastly, I offer my thanks to my family, Trudy, Barton and Paul. My father, Barton Krames, deserves special acknowledgment. He showed that the hard fought lessons in keeping a small shop on Kingsbridge Road solvent and successful apply to organizations far grander in scale. He taught me, in deeds more than words, that there is no substitute for perseverance, hard work, and commitment. He knew each of his customers by name and never refused to deliver an order, even if it meant traveling long distances to do it. By attending to each customer as if his business depended on it, he was able to keep his shop afloat long after most of his competitors closed their doors. I am grateful to him for passing on those timeless lessons. I recognized them quite clearly when I encountered them again in the leadership acts of the CEOs who fill the pages of this book.

SOURCES AND NOTES

As noted in the first part of the book (as well as in the acknowledgments), much of the information for this book came from the CEOs who participated in the preparation of this book. Michael Dell, Herb Kelleher, Lou Gerstner, and David Glass provided invaluable insights that made this a better work. Michael Dell and David Glass were interviewed by phone (a court stenographer was on hand to "record" the interview so that I could focus on the respondents' answers.) Herb Kelleher and Lou Gerstner decided that they could best answer the questions in writing, which indeed did produce most helpful descriptions and analysis of their leadership methods. For the purposes of this section, the date of the "interview" refers to the date that I received their written responses.

In addition to other interviews, more than 250 books, articles, speeches, reports, stock charts, annual reports, and so on were culled and played an important role in the preparation of this book. While the sources of the individual quotes and anecdotes follow, I would like to cite the works that proved most important in providing rich context, historical facts, and insights into the minds and strategies of several of the leaders in the book.

Sam Walton's *Made in America* (New York: Doubleday, 1992) was particularly helpful in the writing of this work, since it contains the most complete description of how Sam Walton built Wal-Mart. As the only book written by Walton, it was invaluable in creating a chapter that captured the essence of his business philosophies and vision, and in giving a voice to an exceptional individual who died more than a decade before the publication of this work.

Andy Grove's *Only the Paranoid Survive* (New York: Currency/Doubleday, 1996) was also an important work that aided in the preparation of this book. While Grove has spoken and written on the subject of strategic inflection points many times throughout the years, this book comprises the most exhaustive knowledge on the subject, straight from Grove himself. It was particularly useful in helping to explain the nuances of strategic inflection points, such as how an organization can help to insulate itself from their threat.

Direct from Dell, by Michael Dell, was a valuable supplement to the lengthy interview that Michael Dell granted this author in early 2002. A concise and candid work, it provided an in-depth discussion of the direct model, and also provided some interesting background material on Dell's life. For example, Dell's explanation of the failure of the product code-named Olympic was gleaned from this leadership memoir.

Other books that proved particularly helpful was *Nuts*, by Kevin and Jackie Freiberg (Bard Press, 1996) which described Herb Kelleher's rich journey at Southwest. Peter Drucker's books are uniformly excellent, and his 1992 publication, *Managing for the Future* (Truman Talley/Dutton Books), was no exception. Robert Slater's books on Jack Welch, from *The New GE* (McGraw-Hill, 1992), to

Jack Welch and the GE Way (McGraw-Hill, 1998), were also instrumental in helping me to advance my own Welch body of knowledge (in the interest of complete disclosure, I edited those works).

THE ERA OF THE CEO?

The *Barron's* piece mentioned in this section was by written by the author and published on October 30, 2000, on the editorial page.

"Advances in excess of $5 million used to be reserved for the Oval Office . . .": Quote by author, in Adam Bryant, "A Neutron Bomb in Bookland," *Newsweek, July 24, 2000*, p. 41.

"There is much talk today that the organization is the enemy . . .": J. Irwin Miller, "The Dilemma of the Corporation Man," *Fortune,* August 1959, p. 102.

"The Imperial Chief Executive Is Suddenly in the Cross Hairs": David Leonhardt, *New York Times,* June 24, 2002, p. 1.

"I've been in business for 40 years . . .": Comment by Andy Grove, in Tim Race's column, *Scandals Appall Some Longtime Chief Executives, New York Times*, July 1, 2002, p. C3.

"Extremely powerful for people in terms of feeling like they actually could do something that was meaningful . . .": Michael Dell, Interview with author, January 10, 2002.

"Grossly misrepresented many aspects of my employment contract": Column by Jack Welch, *Wall Street Journal,* September 16, 2002, editorial page.

CHAPTER 1: THE EXCEPTIONAL SEVEN
AND THE TRAITS THAT DEFINED THEM

Information regarding GE's financial performance appeared in Robert Slater, *The GE Way Fieldbook* (New York: McGraw-Hill, 2000).

". . . that today, in our society, in economics, and in finance . . . ." John C. Bogle, excerpted from his Keynote address, entitled *The Perils of Numeracy*, delivered to The Center for Economic Policy Studies, Princeton University, October 18, 2002.

"The direct model has a number of attributes . . .": Michael Dell, Interview with author, January 10, 2002.

"Build on his legacy and build on his philosophies . . .": David Glass, Interview with author, September 9, 2002.

"Had lost touch with the market . . .": Lou Gerstner, Interview with author, March 21, 2002.

"In the spring of 1993, a big part of what I had to do . . .": ibid.

"Outside-in is a big idea . . .": Jack Welch, speech delivered at 92nd Street Y, New York, New York, March 8, 1999.

"Effective leadership doesn't depend on charisma . . .": Peter Drucker, *The Essential Drucker* (New York: HarperBusiness, 2001), pp. 268–269.

"Mundane, unromantic and boring . . .": Ibid.

"A high-profile, charismatic style is absolutely not required . . .": Jim Collins, *Built to Last* (New York: HarperCollins, 1994), p. 32.

"He probably fits that description more than anyone else I know . . .": David Glass, Interview with author, September 9, 2002.

"Strategically you can make great decisions . . .": Ibid.

"Don't use the abstraction of 'profit' as your goal . . .": Herb Kelleher, Interview with author, January 29, 2002.

"Southwest has many times sacrificed . . .": Ibid.

"One cannot be tentative . . .": Jack Welch, Speech to shareowners, April 22, 1998.

"You have to pretend you're 100% sure. . . .": Andy Grove, "What I've Learned," *Esquire,* May 2000, p. 136.

"The most important role of management . . .": Andy Grove, *Only the Paranoid Survive,* New York: Currency/ Doubleday, 1996, p. 117.

"Culture is one of those things where you know it when you see it . . .": Michael Dell, Interview with author, January 10, 2002.

"Defensiveness is not something that works well within our culture. . . .": Ibid.

"I think it's way underestimated how important the culture has been . . .": David Glass, Interview with author, September 9, 2002.

"Had a good sense for where the ball was going to be . . .": Sam Walton, *Made in America* (New York: Doubleday, 1992), p. 14.

"Oh no, it's happening without us! People are going to write real software for this chip. . . .": Bill Gates, *The Road Ahead* (New York: Times Books, Random House, 1995), p. 16.

"He never stopped trying to do something different. . . .": Bud Walton, quoted in Bob Ortega, *In Sam We Trust* (New York: Times Business, Random House, 1998), pp. 33–48.

"In the twenty-first century . . .": Jack Welch, quoted in Robert Slater's *The New GE,* (New York, McGraw-Hill, 1993), p. 101.

"Have to stop standing on the wrong side of history . . .":
Lou Gerstner, Interview with author, March 21, 2002.

"Where the industry was going to be five or ten years
down the road . . .": ibid.

"Business is ideas and fun and excitement and celebrations,
all those things . . .": Jack Welch, quoted in Janet Lowe,
Jack Welch Speaks (New York: Wiley, 1998), p. 26.

"Sailing's boring. Do you have any idea how much fun it
is to run a billion-dollar company?": Michael Dell,
quoted in Richard Murphy's cover story, , *Success,* January 1999, pp. 50-53.

CHAPTER 2: PLACE THE CUSTOMER AT THE EPICENTER OF THE BUSINESS MODEL

"From the start, our entire business . . .": Michael Dell, *Direct from Dell* (New York: HarperBusiness, 1999), p. 22.

"Being in touch with customer needs . . .": Michael Dell,
Interview with author, January 10, 2002.

"We started the company by building to the customer's
order . . .": Michael Dell, Richard Murphy's cover story,
Success, January 1999, pp. 50-53.

"As a natural extension of customer contact . . .": Michael
Dell, *Direct from Dell*, p. 23.

"We're in the business of dramatically reducing the cost of
distributing technology. . . .": Michael Dell, Andy Serwer, quoted in "Michael Dell Turns the PC World Inside Out," *Fortune*, September 8, 1997, pp. 76-80.

"Hefty profits during the most rapid period of industry
consolidation . . .": Michael Dell, Interview with author, January 10, 2002.

"It goes back to the structural cost advantage . . .": Ibid.

"If you don't have the real ability to differentiate . . .": Ibid.

"Essentially we have now taken on the number one share position . . .": Michael Dell, Interview with author, January 10, 2002.

"First, if you just step back from whether it's direct or indirect . . .": Ibid.

"Be prepared for all possible . . . instances of demand whenever and wherever they may occur . . .": Ibid.

"There are goals to have 100% of our sales on line . . .": Ibid.

"Over 90 percent of our supply chain transactions . . .": Ibid.

"We had gone ahead and created a product . . .": Michael Dell, *Direct from Dell*, p. 39.

"If your business isn't enabled by customers . . .": Michael Dell, Andy Serwer, "Dell's Big New Act," *Fortune*, December 6, 1999, p. 152.

"Teaching bright technical people to think beyond the technology . . .": Michael Dell, *Direct from Dell*, p. 41.

"Segmentation takes the closed feedback loop . . .": Michael Dell, *Direct from Dell*, p. 74.

"Marketing starts with all customers in the market . . .": Peter F. Drucker, *Managing for the Future*, New York: Truman Talley Books/Dutton, 1992, p. 254.

CHAPTER 3: CREATE AN AUTHENTIC LEARNING CULTURE

"Our behavior is driven by a fundamental core belief . . .": Jack Welch, Letter to shareholders, February 7, 1997.

"This boundaryless learning culture killed any view . . .":
Jack Welch, General Electric annual meeting, Charlotte,
N.C., April 23, 1997.

"The hero is the one with the ideas.": Jack Welch, quoted
in Charles R. Day, Jr., and Polly LaBarre, "GE: Just Your
Average Everyday $60 Billion Family Grocery Store,"
Industry Week, May 29, 1994, p. 13.

"Like most American companies, we had built a military
industrial complex . . .": Jack Welch, Interview in
Macleans, November 5, 2001, p. 42.

CHAPTER 4: FOCUS ON SOLUTIONS

"IBM is a solutions company . . .": Lou Gerstner

"So there was IBM . . . :" Louis V. Gerstner, *Who Says Ele-
phants Can't Dance* (New York: HarperCollins, 2002), p. 122.

"It's hard to describe how beaten down that company was":
Andy Grove, quoted in Steve Lohr, "He Loves to Win. At
IBM, He Did," *New York Times*, March 10, 2002, p. 11. b.

"There wasn't going to be an IBM; there was going to
be six or eight IBM's—effectively no IBM . . .": Lou
Gerstner, Interview with author, March 21, 2002.

"Somebody who could sit in the middle of a lot of very-
difficult-to-integrate technology . . .": Ibid.

"The alternative [to breaking up the company] was to keep
IBM together . . .": Lou Gerstner, 1997 shareholders
meeting, Dallas, Texas, April 27, 1997.

"Virtually all the management focus . . .": Lou Gerstner,
Interview with author, March 21, 2002.

"In the spring of 1993, a big part of what I had to do was
get the company refocused on the marketplace . . .":
Lou Gerstner, Interview with author, March 21, 2002.

"One of the key measures that Gerstner took in helping to change the focus from 'inside-out' to 'outside-in' ": The story of Welch addressing top executives at IBM was relayed by Harvey Thompson, a senior IBM executive who attended the meeting, who spoke to this author on September 29, 2002.

"Be patient. By that, I don't mean be complacent..." Lou Gerstner, Interview with author, March 21, 2002.

"We've helped thousands of customers develop a network strategy...": Lou Gerstner, 1998 IBM shareholders conference.

Information regarding IBM's sales and profits performance appeared in Robert Slater, *Saving Big Blue* (New York: McGraw-Hill, 1999).

"Services is the fastest-growing part of the information technology industry...": Lou Gerstner, 1999 IBM shareholders conference.

"The customer would not accept a services company...": Lou Gerstner, quoted by Steve Lohr, "He Loved to Win," *The New York Times*, March 10, 2002, p. 11.

"Set off an incredible bomb in the company...": Ibid.

"Look at technology through the eyes of the customer...": Ibid.

"Every day it becomes more clear that the Net...": Lou Gerstner, IBM web site, December 15, 1999.

Information regarding how the Internet transformed IBM appeared in "IBM: From Big Blue Dinosaur to E-Business Animal," D. Kirkpatrick, *Fortune,* April 26, 1999, p. 116.

"The Internet is ultimately about innovation and integration...": Lou Gerstner, quoted in I. Sager's "Internet Business Machines," *Business Week*, December 13, 1999, p. e30.

Financial data regarding IBM's Internet business appeared in I. Sager's "Internet Business Machines," *Business Week,* December 13, 1999, p. e26. *BW* quotes IT Services Advisory, LLC, Hillside, N.J.

Information regarding Gerstner's decision to keep IBM's research lab in place and focus on solving customers' problems appeared in Robert Slater, *Saving Big Blue* (New York: McGraw-Hill, 1999).

"'If we really believe this, we're going to reprioritize all the budgets in the company. In a period of four weeks . . .'": Lou Gerstner, quoted in "Internet Business Machines," *Business Week,* December 13, 1999, p. e30.

"The real leadership in the industry . . .": Ibid.

CHAPTER 5: PREPARE THE ORGANIZATION
FOR DRASTIC CHANGE

"Most companies don't die because they are wrong . . .": Andy Grove, *Only the Paranoid Survive* (Currency/Doubleday, 1996).

"I submit that all businesses . . .": Andy Grove, Speech to the Irish Information Society Commission, September 20, 1999.

"I have a rule in my business: to see what can happen in the next ten years . . .": Andy Grove, quoted in "Andy Grove on Intel: Magic or Monopoly?" *Upside,* October 12, 1997.

"The essence of a company like Intel is execution and strategy . . .": Ibid.

"You execute on the wrong strategy, you sink . . .": Ibid.

"The need for a different memory strategy . . .": Andy Grove, *Only the Paranoid Survive,* p. 88.

"If we got kicked out and the board brought in a new CEO . . .": Ibid., p. 89.

"We had become marginalized by our Japanese competitors. . . .": Andy Grove, Interview with John Heilemann, *Wired,* June 2001, p. 144.

"For us senior managers, it took the crisis of an economic cycle . . .": Andy Grove, *Only the Paranoid Survive,* p. 97.

"Something has changed, something big, something significant . . .": Ibid., p. 20.

"We managers like to talk about change . . .": Ibid., p. 27.

"We were wandering in the valley of death. . . .": Ibid., p. 89.

"Strategic inflection points offer promises as well as threats. . . .": Ibid., p. 76.

"Businesses are about creating change for other businesses. . . .": Ibid., p. 21.

"I attribute Intel's ability to sustain success to being constantly on the alert . . .": Andy Grove, Chat transcript, October 7, 1996.

"It is best when senior management recognizes and accepts the inevitability . . .": Andy Grove, *Only the Paranoid Survive,* p. 132.

Under *Preparing Your Organization,* the three bold statements in the numbered list are Grove's own wording, from *Only the Paranoid Survive,* pp. 107, 108.

"The prime responsibility of a manager is to guard constantly . . .": Ibid., p. 3.

"Getting through the strategic inflection point required enduring a period of confusion . . .": Ibid., p. 164.

"The dilemma is that you can't suddenly start experimenting . . .": Ibid., p. 130.

"When you are in a strategic transformation . . .": Andy Grove.

CHAPTER 6: HARNESS THE INTELLECT
OF *EVERY* EMPLOYEE

"Smart people anywhere in the company should have the power to drive an initiative": Bill Gates, *Business @ the Speed of Thought* (New York: Warner Books, 1999), p. 16.

"The Internet is not just about new start-up companies. . . .": Bill Gates, "20/20 Vision—A Future for Small Business," Remarks at Sydney Star City Casino, Sydney, Australia, September 11, 2000.

"In time, we named it Microsoft . . .": Bill Gates, *The Road Ahead* (New York: Viking/Penguin Books, 1995), p. 17.

"Our initial insight made everything else a bit easier. . . .": Ibid, p. 18.

"The early dream was a machine that was easy to use . . .": Bill Gates, Remarks at Stanford University, April 25, 2002.

Information regarding Microsoft's court mandates was taken from Forbes.com, September 2002.

"It will allow people to collaborate across the globe. . . .": Bill Gates, "Digital Nervous System—Enterprise Perspective," Speech delivered in New York, March 24, 1999.

"The best tools for empowerment and productivity . . .": Bill Gates, Speech delivered at the Microsoft Research Faculty Summit, Redmond, Wash., July 29, 2002.

"The impact on productivity has been pretty phenomenal. . . .": Bill Gates, Remarks at CEO Summit, May 22, 2002.

"The analogy to the value chain is a good one. . . .": Bill Gates, quoted in "E-Business According to Gates," *Fortune*, April 12, 1999, pp. 72-74.

"Part of this process involves changing the way we buy and sell. . . .": Bill Gates, "20/20 Vision—A Future for Small Business," Remarks at Sydney Star City Casino, Sydney, Australia, September 11, 2000.

"If we go out of business, it won't be because we're not focused on the Internet. . . .": Bill Gates, *Business @ the Speed of Thought*, p. 174.

"Microsoft's awareness that something very dramatic was going on . . .": Bill Gates, Remarks at Georgetown University School of Business, March 24, 1999.

"If we hadn't had electronic mail, and the type of culture that that creates . . .": Ibid.

"Smart people anywhere in the company . . .": Bill Gates, *Business @ the Speed of Thought*, p. 166.

"You very quickly start to get the knowledge workers . . .": Bill Gates, quoted in "E-Business According to Gates," *Fortune*, April 12, 1999, pp. 72-74.

"Actually, there's more effort spent in just impedance . . .": Bill Gates, Remarks at Stanford University, April 25, 2002.

"Your corporate memory is not very good . . .": Bill Gates, "Digital Nervous System—Enterprise Perspective," Speech delivered in New York, March 24, 1999.

CHAPTER 7: CREATE
A PERFORMANCE-DRIVEN CULTURE

"The rule at Southwest is, if somebody has an idea . . .": Herb Kelleher, quoted in Katrina Brooker, "The Chairman of the Board Looks Back," *Fortune,* May 28, 2001, p. 70.

"We try to value each person individually at Southwest . . .": Herb Kelleher, quoted in J. P. Donlan, "Air Herb's Secret Weapon," *Chief Executive,* July-August, 1999, p. 32.

"The culture of Southwest is probably its major competitive advantage. . . .": Herb Kelleher, quoted in Author of Article? "How Herb Keeps Southwest Hopping," *Money,* June 1, 1999, pp. 61-62.

"Thinking like a small company . . .": Herb Kelleher, *Nuts* (Austin, Texas: Bard Press, 1996), p. 78.

"Our esprit de corps is the core of our success. . . .": Herb Kelleher, quoted in "Can Anyone Replace Herb," *Fortune,* April 17, 2000, pp. 186-192.

"If you're an altruistic, outgoing person . . .": Herb Kelleher, quoted in John Huey and Geoffrey Colvin, "The Jack and Herb Show," *Fortune,* January 11, 1999, p. 163.

"We tell our people, 'Don't worry about profit. Think about customer service.' . . .": Herb Kelleher, quoted in J. P. Donlan, "Air Herb's Secret Weapon," *Chief Executive,* July-August 1999, p. 32.

"If you create an environment where the people truly participate . . .": Herb Kelleher, quoted in "A Culture of Commitment," *Leader to Leader,* March 1997.

"I think that even very hardheaded 'managers' . . .": Herb Kelleher, Interview with author, January 29, 2002.

"Culture clash contributes to many of the failures . . .": Ibid.

"Our officers, whom I consider the best in the business, are paid 30 percent less . . .": Herb Kelleher, quoted in "A Culture of Commitment," *Leader to Leader,* March 1997, p. ?.

"We've tried to create an environment where people . . .":
Herb Kelleher, *Nuts*, p. 76.

"The bigger you get, the harder you must continually . . .":
Ibid., p. 77.

Herb Kelleher's thoughts on culture enhancement were
submitted, in writing, in response to questions by the
author, January 29, 2002.

CHAPTER 8: LEARN FROM COMPETITORS,
BUT REMAIN FAITHFUL TO THE VISION

"Most everything I've done . . .": Sam Walton, *Made in
America* (New York: Doubleday, 1992), p. 81.

"At the start we were so amateurish, and so far behind. . . .":
Sam Walton, quoted in Vance H. Trimble, *Sam Walton*
(New York: Dutton, 1990), p. 93.

"Sam's philosophies were really pretty basic . . . ": David
Glass, Interview with author, September 9, 2002.

"What really drove Sam was that competition across the
street . . .": Helen Walton, quoted in Sam Walton, *Made
in America* (New York: Doubleday, 1992), p. 23.

"Most of the best ideas came from our competitors'
stores. . . .": David Glass, Interview with author, September 9, 2002.

"He [Walton] genuinely believed that all of the best ideas
came from the bottom up . . .": Ibid.

"In the whole Wal-Mart scheme of things, the most important contact . . .": Sam Walton, *Made in America*,
p. 128.

"I could never leave well enough alone . . .": Ibid., pp. 27,
47–48.

"What we were obsessed with was keeping our prices below everybody else's. . . .": Ibid., pp. 50–51.

"It's amazing that our competitors didn't catch on to us quicker and try to stop us. . . .": Ibid., pp. 125–126.

"We could really do something with our key strategy . . .": Ibid., p. 109.

"It is much easier to be successful if you have a pretty good competitor . . .": David Glass, Interview with author, September 9, 2002.

"Walton's genius was to recognize that if you have four small towns . . .": Philip Kotler, Interview with author, August 13, 2002.

"There are far more small businesses that go out of business . . .": David Glass, Interview with author, September 9, 2002.

"In Wal-Mart stores they don't want many brands. . . .": Philip Kotler, Interview with author, August 13, 2002.

"If you are going to show the kind of double-digit comparable store sales increases . . .": Sam Walton, *Made in America*, p. 61.

"The first information age CEO. . . .": John Huey, "Discounting Dynamo," in *Time, Builders & Titans* (Time Magazine, special series on Time.com Website.).

"Pouring into Bentonville over phone lines . . .": Sam Walton, *Made in America*, p. 213.

"Some people call Wal-Mart an information company . . .": Philip Kotler, Interview with author, August 13, 2002.

"We used to go through a spiel . . .": David Glass, Interview with author, September 9, 2002.

"By making goods cheap and available . . .": *New York Times,* excerpted from 2001 Wal-Mart annual report.

INDEX